The Two Moors Way
Devon's Coast to Coast Walk
Incorporating The Erme-Plym Trail

Foreword

The Two Moors Way was officially opened on 29th May 1976 between Ivybridge, on the southern edge of Dartmoor, and Lynmouth, on the north coast of Exmoor, by Councillor Ted Pinney, the chairman of Devon County Council's Amenities and Countryside Committee. He unveiled four granite commemorative stones, one at each end and two more along the route, to mark the opening. Since then much of the route has been waymarked, but generally there are no waymarks on open moorland.

The Way links Dartmoor and Exmoor, crossing them both north-south, but it is not just a moorland walk. In the National Parks it passes through a wide variety of scenery. The central section, between the National Parks, while less spectacular, generally has an unspoilt and remote rural feel difficult to find in modern times.

Since 2005 the Two Moors Way has been combined with another route, the Erme-Plym Trail. This latter route links Ivybridge with the South Devon coast, thus creating Devon's Coast to Coast walk.

The County Council has also established a network of recreational footpath routes throughout Devon, linking with each other and with the County's towns and cities. The Devon Coast to Coast is an integral part of that network and has done much to help green tourism.

Because of the long history and public recognition of the Two Moors Way, the name and MW symbol is retained on signposts and waymarkings though it is now part of the Coast to Coast route.

Much of the development and care of the Two Moors Way over the past 30 years was undertaken by individual members of the Two Moors Way Association, notably its late Chairman, Joe Turner, with his wife, Pat. Support from Devon County Council was also important, including production of leaflets and assistance in getting more of the route off the roads. It has now been agreed that the County Council will also undertake responsibility for the production of this guide book. Thanks and appreciation are offered to the Association for all their hard work over the years, not only in providing works on the route but also in the production of the Two Moors Way guide book.

In the Spring of 2004, following the untimely death of Joe Turner, who was interested not only in caring for the Two Moors Way but was the inspiration behind it in the first place, the County Council erected two memorial stones to his memory on the route, near the northern edge of Dartmoor and southern edge of Exmoor. The work of the renowned local sculpture Peter Randall-Page, the stones are formed from a large natural boulder cut in half and inscribed with an almost mesmerising pattern, "facing" each other over some thirty miles of Devon countryside. Make sure you see them and reflect on their significance.

Edward Chorlton
Director of Environment, Economy & Culture and Deputy Chief Executive
Devon County Council

General Introduction

The Devon Coast to Coast walk runs between Wembury on the South Devon coast and Lynmouth on the North Devon coast, passing through two National Parks. It is approximately 187km/117miles long if the route is strictly followed, but in some places there are good or bad weather alternatives and it is unlikely that you will be able to resist diversions to visit places of interest nearby. So be prepared for a somewhat longer walk. Take it slowly and enjoy yourself.

The terrain is varied with stretches of open moor, deep wooded river valleys, green lanes and minor roads. Much of the route is hilly, so the distances you plan to walk must take this into account. Though an active rambler may be able to complete the walk in a few days, the majority will need longer, even a full fortnight, especially if the richness of the countryside, its antiquities, churches and many other historic buildings, as well as its panoramic views, are all to be appreciated.

Archaeology and Traditional Buildings

Dartmoor has more Prehistoric remains that any other National Park in Europe. These include cairns, kists, menhirs and stone rows as well as hut circles and enclosures. Such remains are also to be found on Exmoor.

Much use was made of granite in the 15th - 17th centuries. It is found on farms as well as churches and great houses as door and window frames, troughs and grind-stones. It is particularly noticeable at Castle Drogo, the last castle built in England, passed along the Way on the northern edge of Dartmoor.

Roughcast rubble and cob is also common, particularly in Mid Devon. Cob consists of a mix of stiff clay compacted with chopped straw and seems to have been known in Devon since the 13th century. Though the art of using it as a building material died out about 1850, there has been a recent revival as a rural skill and it is being used for appropriate renovation work. On average cob walls are about 3ft thick, though sometimes they are as much as 4ft 6in. Usually the thicker the wall the older the building. Raw cob is sandy to reddish brown but both it and roughcast or plastered rubble are often colour-washed as protection from the weather.

Cob deteriorates rapidly if rain gets in from the top, so even walls which are not parts of buildings have slate or thatch coping. When cob goes down to ground level there is often a tarred strip along the bottom. In older houses, brick is seldom used except for chimney stacks.

Woodlands and Hedges

The native woodlands are mainly oak or ash, but coniferous plantations have encroached on the landscape in places. Though not intrinsically ugly, they offend the Devon purist. Fortunately elm was never a dominant tree, so that the depredations of Dutch elm disease are not conspicuous.

The typical Devon hedge has a core of stones built up with turf so that it very soon appears as a solid bank on top of which grow shrubs and even full-sized trees. In many places hedges were removed to make the fields larger and ease the handling of machinery, but there is now some doubt if this is wise because of erosion, which wire and wooden fencing does nothing to impede. Hedges often reduce the view but they provide a wealth of interesting wayside flowers and wildlife.

Walking the Route

Before you set out, read through the overview notes for the sections of the route. These will tell you the type of country to expect and give some guidance about access to the area. You will also find brief notes, referring to the features you will pass on the individual maps. These are not exhaustive and you will probably wish to read more in specific books and guides obtainable locally at places of interest.

Accommodation

Devon County Council does not hold a comprehensive recommended list of accommodation on the Devon Coast to Coast walk. The Two Moors Way Association will provide information on the whole Coast to Coast route; send £2 plus a s.a.e. to the Two Moors Way Association, 63 Higher Coombe Drive, Teignmouth, Devon TQ14 9NL. Note that a packhorse system for transport of luggage is available between many of the places listed. Details are available with the accommodation list.

Signs and Waymarks

The Erme-Plym Trail logo marks the route between Wembury and Ivybridge, while on the Two Moors Way the MW logo is used. However the open moorland of Dartmoor and Exmoor is NOT signposted or waymarked. Not only is marking alien to the wild landscape, but it destroys the experience of being in remote country. The walker may roam freely on access land, tinted pale green on the relevant maps.

The scale of the maps is approximately 1:18,000. A Grid North on each page will help when taking compass bearings. Grid references are given in the margins. The grid intervals of 1 km can be used to estimate distances, 1km = ⁵⁄₈ mile.

The maps are numbered. The north-bound traveller should read straight through the book, while the south-bound should read the overview and then turn to the back and read backwards. Specific written instructions are only given to clarify points where confusion can arise.

Map key

.... general direction on open ground

- - - - - - - - - - - - - - - - - - footpaths

::::::::::::::::::::::::::: unfenced roads

= = = = = = = = = = : fenced tracks and green lanes

= = = = = = = = = = : unfenced tracks

═══════════════ fenced roads

──────────── Main walk route

● ● ● ● ● ● ● ● Alternative walk route

        Access land (Countryside and Rights of Way Act 2000)

Based upon the Ordnance Survey Maps
with sanction of the Controller of
Her Majesty's Stationery Office,
Crown copyright reserved.

Some Ancient Waymarkers

Hangershell Rock

Hamel Down Cross

Hobajohn's Cross

Bennett's Cross

Huntingdon Cross

Devon Coast to Coast Map

Lynmouth **14**

South West Coast Path & Tarka Trail

South West Coast Path

13

Simonsbath **12**

Bristol Channel

Exmoor National Park

Barnstaple

Tarka Trail

11 West Anstey

Exe Valley Way

Ridge and Valley link to Tarka Trail

Witheridge

D E V O N

10

Morchard Bishop

Devonshire Heartland Way

Devonshire Heartland Way

Two Moors Way

Erme-Plym Trail

Link paths

9

Dartmoor Way & Taw-Teign link to Tarka Trail

8

Drewsteignton

Exeter

Dartmoor Way

Dartmoor National Park

7

6

Dartmoor Way

Widecombe-in-the-Moor

English Channel

5

4 Dartmoor Way

South West Coast Path

Plymouth

West Devon Way

2

3 Ivybridge

Torbay

1

Wembury

South West Coast Path

Overview of the Route

The Erme-Plym Trail

1 **Wembury**

Wembury is an attractive village on Devon's south coast to the east of Plymouth. The start and finish of Devon's Coast to Coast is Wembury Beach, adjacent to the Old Mill Cafe where there is a signing-in book during opening hours (check 01752 862314 for details). The village is linked to Plymouth city centre by a regular bus service.

2 **Wembury - Ivybridge**   Maps: `N1-5` `S35-39`

Distance 24km/15 miles

This is a generally gentle undulating stretch over an attractive pastoral landscape. Views of Dartmoor dominate the northern skyline. A particular highlight is the crossing of Cofflete Creek, a tributary of the estuary of the River Yealm. After passing through the attractive villages of Brixton and Yealmpton the northbound route reaches the Erme Valley which is followed into Ivybridge.

The Two Moors Way

3 **Ivybridge**

Ivybridge enjoys both a magnificent natural setting and centuries of history as a mill town and a staging post on the London road from Plymouth. Situated on the banks of the River Erme the town provides a range of facilities. There are good bus services from Exeter, Plymouth and Torbay with connections to long distance services. There is also a railway station served by connecting trains travelling between Plymouth and Exeter.

4 **Ivybridge -Scorriton**   Maps: `N6-10` `S30-34`

Distance 19km/12 miles

After leaving Ivybridge the route is entirely across uninhabited open moorland with virtually no shelter. This section of the Way is scattered with Bronze Age remains in the form of hut circles, enclosures, cairns, kists and stone rows such as are described in Worth's Dartmoor. There are remains of the mining activity on Erme Plains and in the Huntingdon Warren area and disused china clay workings at Leftlake and also a short distance from the route at Redlake. The track of the Redlake tramway is a good guide when crossing Ugborough Moor in poor visibility. Between the tramway and Scorriton care is needed in navigating, especially in poor visibility.

5 Scorriton - Jordan

Maps: N11-12 S28-29

Distance 17km/11 miles

This is a very hilly section of the route, crossing the valleys of the Holy Brook and the Dart and climbing up onto the moor to cross Sherberton Common before dropping into the valley of the West Webburn. New Bridge, a narrow mediaeval structure, carries the road from Princetown via Dartmeet to Ashburton. With the exception of Holne, which has a pub and shop, the villages in this area are little more than hamlets.

6 Jordan - Mariners' Way

Maps: N13-15 S25-27

Distance 16km/10 miles

Much of this section of the route is over moor but never too far from roads. The B3212, which is crossed about 1km east of the Warren House Inn, is the main road across Dartmoor from Plymouth or Tavistock to Exeter via Moretonhampstead. There is a bus service in summer and at weekends in winter. Travellers wishing to use the Bellever Youth Hostel leave the route here and go via Postbridge or can turn west at Jordan Mill or at the next cross-roads to the north.

Widecombe-in-the-Moor is worth a visit and the route can be rejoined without any retracing of steps by by-passing a piece of open moor. It is the only village on or near this part of the route.

7 The Mariners' Way

Map: N16 S24

Distance 4km/2.5 miles

Between Yardworthy and Teigncombe the Two Moors Way uses a short section of the Mariners' Way. This once led from Dartmouth to Bideford, but only part of the Dartmoor stretch can now be identified.

8 Teigncombe - Drewsteignton   Maps: N16-18 S22-24

Distance 10 km/6 miles

The greater part of this section of the route lies in the valley of the River Teign. It is necessary to follow lanes as far as Chagford Bridge, but the rest of the way is by paths beside the water or at higher level below Castle Drogo, with a short stretch of high undulating ground near Drewsteignton village. There is a bus service from Okehampton to Exeter and also to Bovey Tracey via Chagford and Moretonhampstead. The A382, crossed at Dogmarsh Bridge, is the main road from Okehampton to Bovey Tracey.

9 Drewsteignton - Morchard Bishop   Maps: N18-23 S17-22

Distance 24km/15 miles

The A30, 1.7km north of Drewsteignton, marks the boundary of the Dartmoor National Park. Thus the greater part of this section of the route is in the Mid Devon area.

Undulating agricultural land is networked with well waymarked narrow lanes and footpaths. The northward way has some easting. The route crosses the A30, A3072 and A377 roads and also the Exeter-Okehampton and Exeter-Barnstaple branch railway lines. The former line is closed to passenger trains, except on summer Sundays, but the latter is still open with a station at Morchard Road. There is a reasonable bus service on the old A30 between Okehampton and Exeter and also on the A377 between Exeter, Crediton and Barnstaple.

10 Morchard Bishop - Hawkridge   Maps: N23-31 S9-17

Distance 36km/22 miles

The route passes through farming country, with Dartmoor and Exmoor visible on the horizons. While keeping in the main to high ground, it dips into a number of valleys to cross small rivers which drain westwards into the Taw.

Witheridge is the only place of any size along the Way. Situated on the B3137, it has buses to Tiverton and Barnstaple. There are also buses between Taunton and Barnstaple on the A3227 south of Yeo Mill.

The boundary of the Exmoor National Park runs just north of West Anstey, while the Dane's Brook at Slade divides Somerset from Devon.

11 Hawkridge - Withypool

Maps: N31-32 S8-9

Distance 11km/7 miles

The preferred route follows the River Barle, keeping to its east bank trough a beautiful wooded valley but, after exceptionally wet weather, Tarr Steps may be flooded and impassable and the alternative, somewhat shorter route, over Parsonage Down and the shoulder of Withypool Hill should be used.

From the Dulverton road just out of Withypool there is a footpath to the Exford Youth Hostel. Withypool has a pub and shops.

12 Withypool - Hoar Oak

Maps: N33-37 S3-7

Distance 19km/12 miles

The Way keeps mainly to high ground with dips to cross and recross the River Barle. It is for the most part uninhabited, with Simonsbath being the only settlement. The path into the village beside the River Barle is a particular highlight.

13 Hoar Oak - Lynmouth

Maps: N37-39 S1-3

Distance 10km/6 miles

The Way runs approximately north/south over the open moor of Cheriton Ridge, with wide views on either side. It then follows a lane to Scoresdown.

Near Smallcombe Bridge the route enters a wood through Combe Park, National Trust property to Combe Park Lodge near Hillsford Bridge. After crossing the A39, the Way climbs to follow the spectacular high level path along the Cleaves above the East Lyn River. The final descent to Lynmouth is very steep.

14 Lynmouth

Lynmouth, at the northern end of the Two Moors Way, is virtually one town with Lynton. The houses cluster on the steep sides of the East and West Lyn Rivers and along the coastal strip. The area is very popular with summer visitors and has holiday accommodation and other services as well as a Youth Hostel at Lynbridge, a short distance up the valley of the West Lyn. There is a range of facilities in Lynmouth and a signing in book at the Glen Lyn Gorge, signposted in the town.

Mileage Chart

Erme-Plym Trail	km	miles
Wembury - Brixton	8	5
Brixton - Yealmpton	3.25	2
Yealmpton - Sequer's Bridge (A379)	6.75	4.25
Sequer's Bridge (A379) - Ivybridge	6	4.75

Two Moors Way		
Ivybridge - Holne	24	15
Holne - Hameldown (for Widecombe)	12.75	8
Hameldown (for Widecombe) - Chagford	17.5	11
Chagford - Drewsteignton	6.5	4
Drewsteignton - Morchard Bishop	25.5	16
Morchard Bishop - Witheridge	12.75	8
Witheridge - Knowstone	12.75	8
Knowstone - Hawkridge	12.75	8
Hawkridge - Withypool	9.5	6
Withypool - Simonsbath	11	7
Simonsbath - Lynmouth	19.25	12

Relics of the Tin Industry

Quickbeam tin workings and viaduct
for Redlake china clay pipe line

Ruined tinners' hut
- Erme Pound

Mortar Stone

Stone with broken mould, polished axle
socket and slot for a stamp frame
- Hecklake

Mould stone - reused
in wall near Dockwell

Ruins of a blowing house
- used as a chapel by the Rev. Keble Martin

Public Transport and Facilities

For bus timetable details telephone Traveline on
0870 608 2 608 **or visit** www.traveline.org.uk

For train timetables call the National Rail Enquiries line on
08457 484950 **or visit** www.thetrainline.com

Wembury
Buses to and from Plymouth

Brixton
Buses to and from Plymouth or Dartmouth

Yealmpton
Buses to and from Plymouth or Dartmouth

Ivybridge
Buses to and from Plymouth, Exeter and Torbay
Trains to and from Plymouth and Exeter
(and sometimes further afield)

Scorriton

Holne

New Bridge

Widecombe (1.25miles/2kms off route)

Bennett's Cross
Buses to and from Plymouth and Exeter

Warren House (0.6miles/1km off route)

Chagford (0.6miles/1km off route)
Buses to and from Exeter and Okehampton

Drewsteignton
Buses to and from Exeter and Okehampton

Morchard Road
Buses to and from Exeter and Barnstaple
Trains to and from Exeter and Barnstaple ◖ WC

Morchard Bishop
Buses to and from Exeter 🏠 ◖

Witheridge
Buses to and from Tiverton Parkway (railway station),
Tiverton and Barnstaple 🏠 ◖ WC

Knowstone ◖

B3227 (between Knowstone and West Anstey)
Buses to and from Barnstaple and Taunton

Yeo Mill 🏠 WC

Tarr Steps ✗ WC

Withypool ✗ 🏠 ◖

Simonsbath ✗ ◖ WC

Watersmeet (0.6miles/1km off route) ✗ 🏠 WC

Lynmouth
Buses to and from Barnstaple, Minehead and Taunton
Certain other locations may have occasional services
on certain days of the week only. ℹ(Lynton) ✗ 🏠 ◖ WC

Guide to Symbols

✗ Café   🏠 Shops   ◖ Pub   WC Toilets
ℹ Information Centre

15

Relevant Ordnance Survey Maps

Landranger

201 Plymouth and Launceston (Wembury - Brixton)
202 Torbay and South Dartmoor (Brixton - Mel Tor)
191 Okehampton and North Dartmoor (Mel Tor - Washford Pyne)
181 Minehead and Brendon Hills (Washford Pyne - Landacre)
180 Barnstaple and Ilfracombe (Landacre - Lynmouth)

Explorer (NB there is some overlap)

OL20 South Devon (Wembury - Crossways)
OL28 Dartmoor (Ivybridge -Hittisleigh)
113 Okehampton (Drewsteignton - Black Dog)
127 South Molton and Chudleigh (Black Dog (2km only))
114 Exeter and the Exe Valley (Black Dog - West Anstey Common)
OL9 Exmoor (West Anstey - Lynmouth)

Special Stones

Dartmoor especially is renowned for the wealth of stones, ranging from the prehistoric to the mediaeval and later. However, this route has further stones which add to the range.

At the opening of the Two Moors Way in 1976, four commemorative granite stones were unveiled and those are still in place. Look out for them on the Way, now quite weather-worn, at Ivybridge, Drewsteignton, Morchard Bishop and Lynmouth.

Extra Special Stones

In the spring of 2004 occurred the untimely death of Joe Turner, a local rambler and amateur archaeologist who was responsible for both inspiring the Two Moors Way and also establishing it, as well as for many years helping to maintain it. The local authorities agreed that appropriate stones would be the most fitting memorial. The renowned local sculptor, Peter Randall-Page, created the memorial out of a river washed granite boulder. The stone was cut in half and an innovative natural design was inscribed on the cut faces. The two mirror-image half-boulders were then placed "facing" each other over some 30 miles of Devon countryside, on the northern edge of Dartmoor near Drewsteignton and the southern edge of Exmoor near West Anstey. Near each is a small stone explanatory plaque. Make sure you see the stones - run your hand over the faces and let them speak to you!

Extra Special Stones

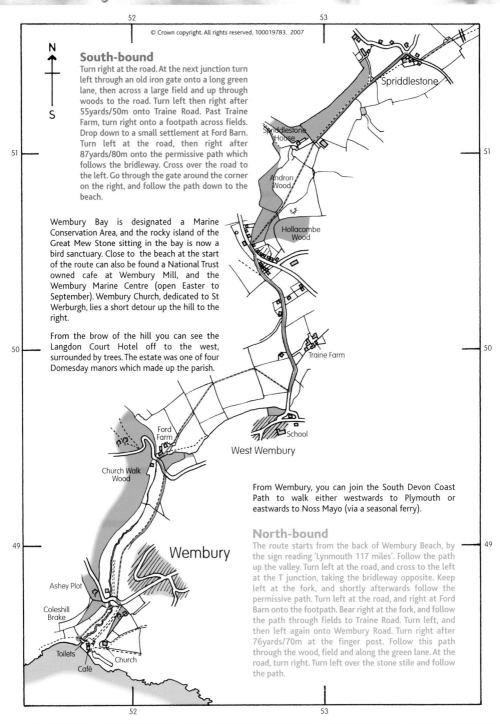

52   53

N
↑
|
S

Spriddlestone

Spriddlestone House

Andron Wood

Hollacombe Wood

Traine Farm

Ford Farm

School

West Wembury

Church Walk Wood

Wembury

Ashey Plot

Coleshill Brake

Toilets

Church

Café

51   51
50   50
49   49
52   53

South-bound

Turn right at the road. At the next junction turn left through an old iron gate onto a long green lane, then across a large field and up through woods to the road. Turn left then right after 55yards/50m onto Traine Road. Past Traine Farm, turn right onto a footpath across fields. Drop down to a small settlement at Ford Barn. Turn left at the road, then right after 87yards/80m onto the permissive path which follows the bridleway. Cross over the road to the left. Go through the gate around the corner on the right, and follow the path down to the beach.

Wembury Bay is designated a Marine Conservation Area, and the rocky island of the Great Mew Stone sitting in the bay is now a bird sanctuary. Close to the beach at the start of the route can also be found a National Trust owned cafe at Wembury Mill, and the Wembury Marine Centre (open Easter to September). Wembury Church, dedicated to St Werburgh, lies a short detour up the hill to the right.

From the brow of the hill you can see the Langdon Court Hotel off to the west, surrounded by trees. The estate was one of four Domesday manors which made up the parish.

From Wembury, you can join the South Devon Coast Path to walk either westwards to Plymouth or eastwards to Noss Mayo (via a seasonal ferry).

North-bound

The route starts from the back of Wembury Beach, by the sign reading 'Lynmouth 117 miles'. Follow the path up the valley. Turn left at the road, and cross to the left at the T junction, taking the bridleway opposite. Keep left at the fork, and shortly afterwards follow the permissive path. Turn left at the road, and right at Ford Barn onto the footpath. Bear right at the fork, and follow the path through fields to Traine Road. Turn left, and then left again onto Wembury Road. Turn right after 76yards/70m at the finger post. Follow this path through the wood, field and along the green lane. At the road, turn right. Turn left over the stone stile and follow the path.

N1 S38

See key to maps on page 7

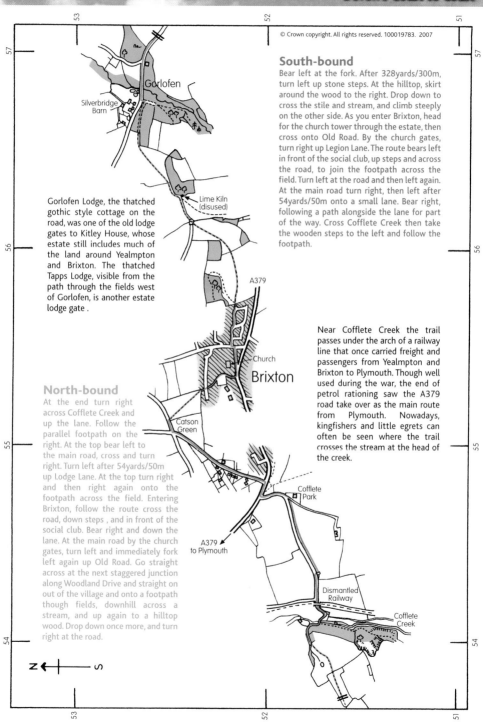

South-bound

Bear left at the fork. After 328yards/300m, turn left up stone steps. At the hilltop, skirt around the wood to the right. Drop down to cross the stile and stream, and climb steeply on the other side. As you enter Brixton, head for the church tower through the estate, then cross onto Old Road. By the church gates, turn right up Legion Lane. The route bears left in front of the social club, up steps and across the road, to join the footpath across the field. Turn left at the road and then left again. At the main road turn right, then left after 54yards/50m onto a small lane. Bear right, following a path alongside the lane for part of the way. Cross Cofflete Creek then take the wooden steps to the left and follow the footpath.

Gorlofen Lodge, the thatched gothic style cottage on the road, was one of the old lodge gates to Kitley House, whose estate still includes much of the land around Yealmpton and Brixton. The thatched Tapps Lodge, visible from the path through the fields west of Gorlofen, is another estate lodge gate .

Near Cofflete Creek the trail passes under the arch of a railway line that once carried freight and passengers from Yealmpton and Brixton to Plymouth. Though well used during the war, the end of petrol rationing saw the A379 road take over as the main route from Plymouth. Nowadays, kingfishers and little egrets can often be seen where the trail crosses the stream at the head of the creek.

North-bound

At the end turn right across Cofflete Creek and up the lane. Follow the parallel footpath on the right. At the top bear left to the main road, cross and turn right. Turn left after 54yards/50m up Lodge Lane. At the top turn right and then right again onto the footpath across the field. Entering Brixton, follow the route cross the road, down steps , and in front of the social club. Bear right and down the lane. At the main road by the church gates, turn left and immediately fork left again up Old Road. Go straight across at the next staggered junction along Woodland Drive and straight on out of the village and onto a footpath though fields, downhill across a stream, and up again to a hilltop wood. Drop down once more, and turn right at the road.

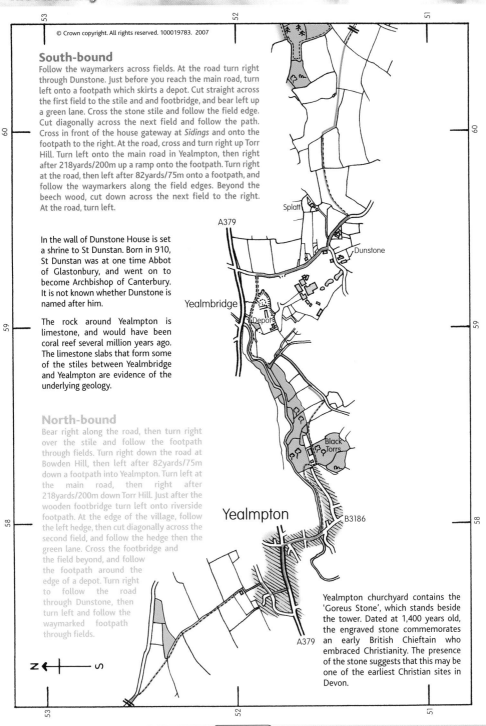

South-bound

Follow the waymarkers across fields. At the road turn right through Dunstone. Just before you reach the main road, turn left onto a footpath which skirts a depot. Cut straight across the first field to the stile and and footbridge, and bear left up a green lane. Cross the stone stile and follow the field edge. Cut diagonally across the next field and follow the path. Cross in front of the house gateway at *Sidings* and onto the footpath to the right. At the road, cross and turn right up Torr Hill. Turn left onto the main road in Yealmpton, then right after 218yards/200m up a ramp onto the footpath. Turn right at the road, then left after 82yards/75m onto a footpath, and follow the waymarkers along the field edges. Beyond the beech wood, cut down across the next field to the right. At the road, turn left.

In the wall of Dunstone House is set a shrine to St Dunstan. Born in 910, St Dunstan was at one time Abbot of Glastonbury, and went on to become Archbishop of Canterbury. It is not known whether Dunstone is named after him.

The rock around Yealmpton is limestone, and would have been coral reef several million years ago. The limestone slabs that form some of the stiles between Yealmbridge and Yealmpton are evidence of the underlying geology.

North-bound

Bear right along the road, then turn right over the stile and follow the footpath through fields. Turn right down the road at Bowden Hill, then left after 82yards/75m down a footpath into Yealmpton. Turn left at the main road, then right after 218yards/200m down Torr Hill. Just after the wooden footbridge turn left onto riverside footpath. At the edge of the village, follow the left hedge, then cut diagonally across the second field, and follow the hedge then the green lane. Cross the footbridge and the field beyond, and follow the footpath around the edge of a depot. Turn right to follow the road through Dunstone, then turn left and follow the waymarked footpath through fields.

Yealmpton churchyard contains the 'Goreus Stone', which stands beside the tower. Dated at 1,400 years old, the engraved stone commemorates an early British Chieftain who embraced Christianity. The presence of the stone suggests that this may be one of the earliest Christian sites in Devon.

N3   S36

See key to maps on page 7

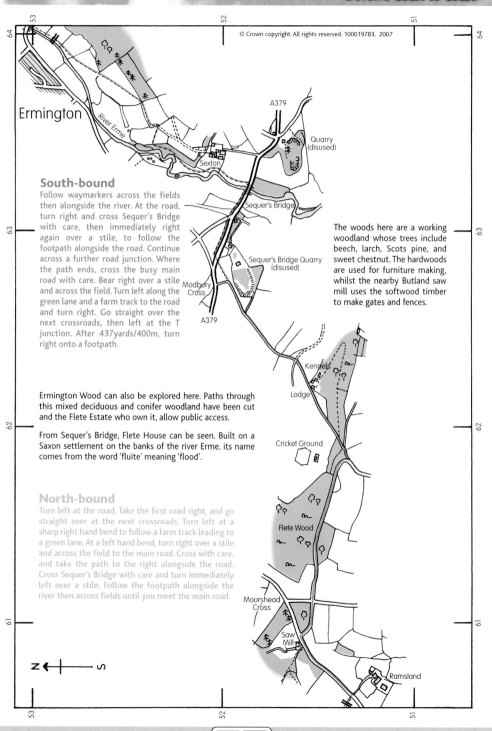

South-bound

Follow waymarkers across the fields then alongside the river. At the road, turn right and cross Sequer's Bridge with care, then immediately right again over a stile, to follow the footpath alongside the road. Continue across a further road junction. Where the path ends, cross the busy main road with care. Bear right over a stile and across the field. Turn left along the green lane and a farm track to the road and turn right. Go straight over the next crossroads, then left at the T junction. After 437yards/400m, turn right onto a footpath.

The woods here are a working woodland whose trees include beech, larch, Scots pine, and sweet chestnut. The hardwoods are used for furniture making, whilst the nearby Butland saw mill uses the softwood timber to make gates and fences.

Ermington Wood can also be explored here. Paths through this mixed deciduous and conifer woodland have been cut and the Flete Estate who own it, allow public access.

From Sequer's Bridge, Flete House can be seen. Built on a Saxon settlement on the banks of the river Erme, its name comes from the word 'fluite' meaning 'flood'.

North-bound

Turn left at the road. Take the first road right, and go straight over at the next crossroads. Turn left at a sharp right hand bend to follow a farm track leading to a green lane. At a left hand bend, turn right over a stile and across the field to the main road. Cross with care, and take the path to the right alongside the road. Cross Sequer's Bridge with care and turn immediately left over a stile. Follow the footpath alongside the river then across fields until you meet the main road.

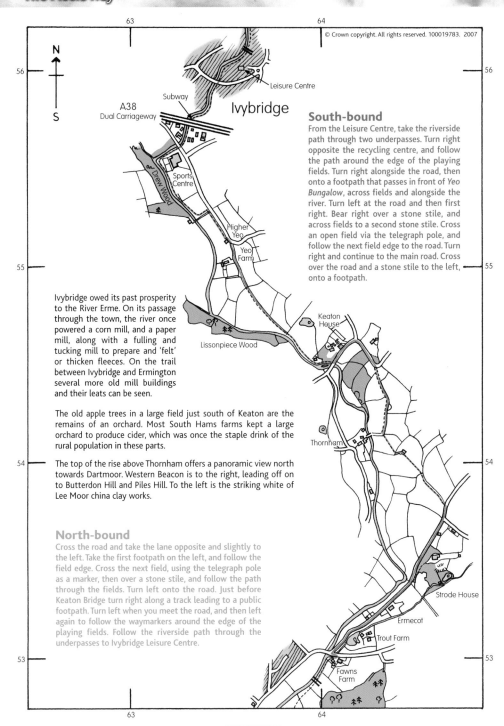

Ivybridge

Leisure Centre

Subway

A38
Dual Carriageway

N

S

Drew Wood

Sports
Centre

Higher
Yeo

Yeo
Farm

Keaton
House

Lissonpiece Wood

Thornham

Strode House

Ermecot

Trout Farm

Fawns
Farm

South-bound

From the Leisure Centre, take the riverside path through two underpasses. Turn right opposite the recycling centre, and follow the path around the edge of the playing fields. Turn right alongside the road, then onto a footpath that passes in front of *Yeo Bungalow*, across fields and alongside the river. Turn left at the road and then first right. Bear right over a stone stile, and across fields to a second stone stile. Cross an open field via the telegraph pole, and follow the next field edge to the road. Turn right and continue to the main road. Cross over the road and a stone stile to the left, onto a footpath.

Ivybridge owed its past prosperity to the River Erme. On its passage through the town, the river once powered a corn mill, and a paper mill, along with a fulling and tucking mill to prepare and 'felt' or thicken fleeces. On the trail between Ivybridge and Ermington several more old mill buildings and their leats can be seen.

The old apple trees in a large field just south of Keaton are the remains of an orchard. Most South Hams farms kept a large orchard to produce cider, which was once the staple drink of the rural population in these parts.

The top of the rise above Thornham offers a panoramic view north towards Dartmoor. Western Beacon is to the right, leading off on to Butterdon Hill and Piles Hill. To the left is the striking white of Lee Moor china clay works.

North-bound

Cross the road and take the lane opposite and slightly to the left. Take the first footpath on the left, and follow the field edge. Cross the next field, using the telegraph pole as a marker, then over a stone stile, and follow the path through the fields. Turn left onto the road. Just before Keaton Bridge turn right along a track leading to a public footpath. Turn left when you meet the road, and then left again to follow the waymarkers around the edge of the playing fields. Follow the riverside path through the underpasses to Ivybridge Leisure Centre.

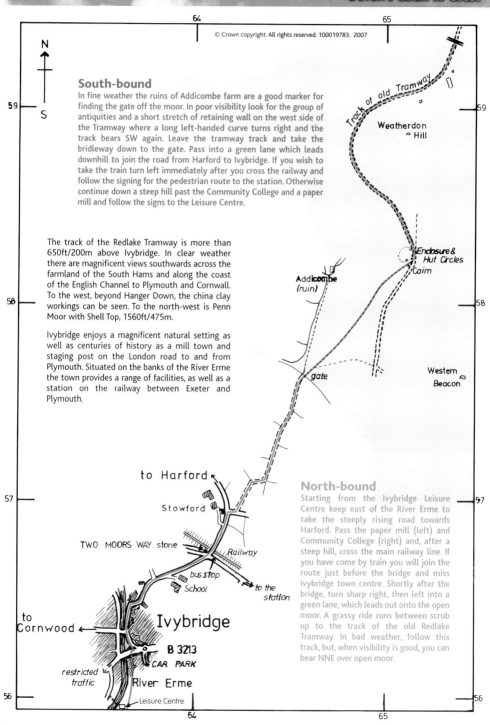

© Crown copyright. All rights reserved. 100019783. 2007

South-bound

In fine weather the ruins of Addicombe farm are a good marker for finding the gate off the moor. In poor visibility look for the group of antiquities and a short stretch of retaining wall on the west side of the Tramway where a long left-handed curve turns right and the track bears SW again. Leave the tramway track and take the bridleway down to the gate. Pass into a green lane which leads downhill to join the road from Harford to Ivybridge. If you wish to take the train turn left immediately after you cross the railway and follow the signing for the pedestrian route to the station. Otherwise continue down a steep hill past the Community College and a paper mill and follow the signs to the Leisure Centre.

The track of the Redlake Tramway is more than 650ft/200m above Ivybridge. In clear weather there are magnificent views southwards across the farmland of the South Hams and along the coast of the English Channel to Plymouth and Cornwall. To the west, beyond Hanger Down, the china clay workings can be seen. To the north-west is Penn Moor with Shell Top, 1560ft/475m.

Ivybridge enjoys a magnificent natural setting as well as centuries of history as a mill town and staging post on the London road to and from Plymouth. Situated on the banks of the River Erme the town provides a range of facilities, as well as a station on the railway between Exeter and Plymouth.

North-bound

Starting from the Ivybridge Leisure Centre keep east of the River Erme to take the steeply rising road towards Harford. Pass the paper mill (left) and Community College (right) and, after a steep hill, cross the main railway line. If you have come by train you will join the route just before the bridge and miss Ivybridge town centre. Shortly after the bridge, turn sharp right, then left into a green lane, which leads out onto the open moor. A grassy ride runs between scrub up to the track of the old Redlake Tramway. In bad weather, follow this track, but, when visibility is good, you can bear NNE over open moor.

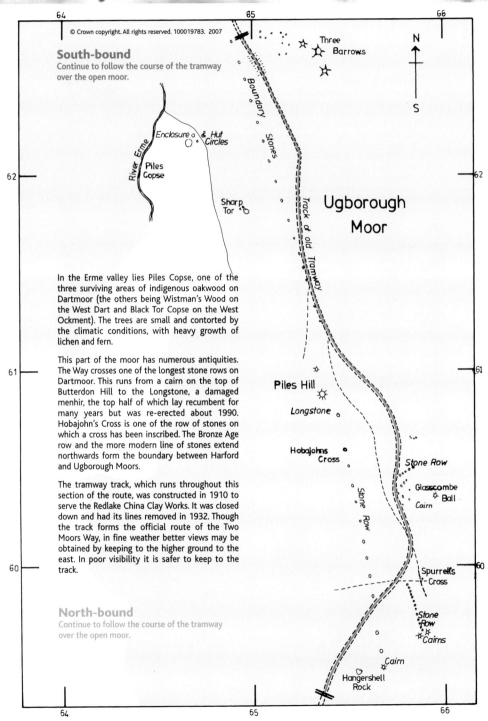

© Crown copyright. All rights reserved. 100019783. 2007

South-bound
Continue to follow the course of the tramway over the open moor.

Three Barrows

N
S

Boundary Stones

River Erme

Enclosure & Hut Circles

Piles Copse

Sharp Tor

Track of old Tramway

Ugborough Moor

In the Erme valley lies Piles Copse, one of the three surviving areas of indigenous oakwood on Dartmoor (the others being Wistman's Wood on the West Dart and Black Tor Copse on the West Ockment). The trees are small and contorted by the climatic conditions, with heavy growth of lichen and fern.

This part of the moor has numerous antiquities. The Way crosses one of the longest stone rows on Dartmoor. This runs from a cairn on the top of Butterdon Hill to the Longstone, a damaged menhir, the top half of which lay recumbent for many years but was re-erected about 1990. Hobajohn's Cross is one of the row of stones on which a cross has been inscribed. The Bronze Age row and the more modern line of stones extend northwards form the boundary between Harford and Ugborough Moors.

The tramway track, which runs throughout this section of the route, was constructed in 1910 to serve the Redlake China Clay Works. It was closed down and had its lines removed in 1932. Though the track forms the official route of the Two Moors Way, in fine weather better views may be obtained by keeping to the higher ground to the east. In poor visibility it is safer to keep to the track.

Piles Hill

Longstone

Hobajohns Cross

Stone Row

Glasscombe Ball

Cairn

Stone Row

Spurrell's Cross

Stone Row Cairns

North-bound
Continue to follow the course of the tramway over the open moor.

Cairn

Cairn

Hangershell Rock

N7 S32

See key to maps on page 7

Bronze Age Antiquities

Double stone row - Chagford Common

Hut circle - North Bovey Head

Hamel Down kistvaen

Grimspound

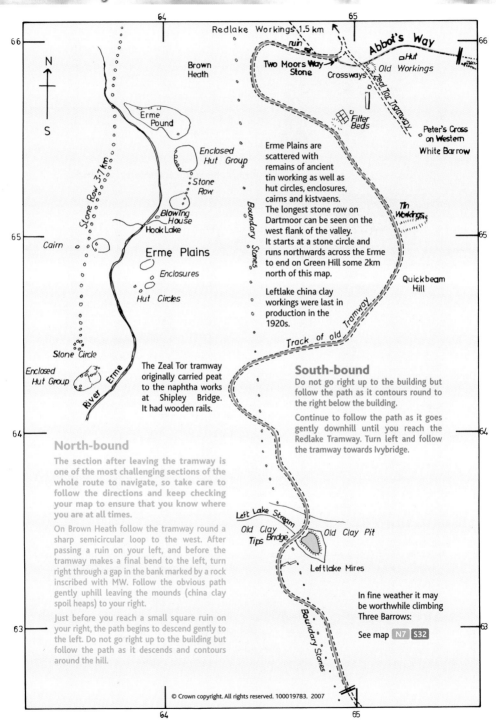

Redlake Workings 1.5 km

ruin

Abbot's Way

Brown Heath

Two Moors Way Stone

Crossways

□Hut

Old Workings

Zeal Tor Tramway

Filter Beds

Peter's Cross on Western

White Barrow

Erme Pound

Enclosed Hut Group

Stone Row

Stone Row 3.7 km

Blowing House

Hook Lake

Boundary Stones

Erme Plains

Cairn

Enclosures

Hut Circles

Erme Plains are scattered with remains of ancient tin working as well as hut circles, enclosures, cairns and kistvaens.
The longest stone row on Dartmoor can be seen on the west flank of the valley.
It starts at a stone circle and runs northwards across the Erme to end on Green Hill some 2km north of this map.

Tin Workings

Quickbeam Hill

Leftlake china clay workings were last in production in the 1920s.

Track of old Tramway

Stone Circle

Enclosed Hut Group

River Erme

The Zeal Tor tramway originally carried peat to the naphtha works at Shipley Bridge. It had wooden rails.

South-bound

Do not go right up to the building but follow the path as it contours round to the right below the building.

Continue to follow the path as it goes gently downhill until you reach the Redlake Tramway. Turn left and follow the tramway towards Ivybridge.

North-bound

The section after leaving the tramway is one of the most challenging sections of the whole route to navigate, so take care to follow the directions and keep checking your map to ensure that you know where you are at all times.

On Brown Heath follow the tramway round a sharp semicircular loop to the west. After passing a ruin on your left, and before the tramway makes a final bend to the left, turn right through a gap in the bank marked by a rock inscribed with MW. Follow the obvious path gently uphill leaving the mounds (china clay spoil heaps) to your right.

Just before you reach a small square ruin on your right, the path begins to descend gently to the left. Do not go right up to the building but follow the path as it descends and contours around the hill.

Left Lake Stream

Old Clay Tips

Bridge

Old Clay Pit

Leftlake Mires

Boundary Stones

In fine weather it may be worthwhile climbing Three Barrows:

See map N7 S32

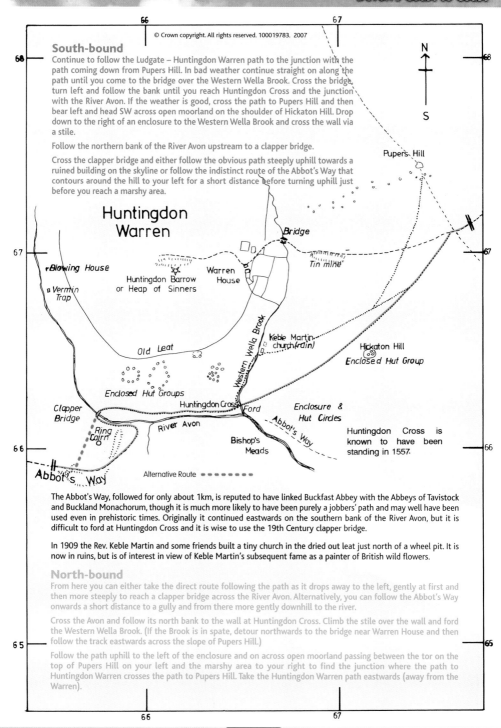

South-bound

Continue to follow the Ludgate – Huntingdon Warren path to the junction with the path coming down from Pupers Hill. In bad weather continue straight on along the path until you come to the bridge over the Western Wella Brook. Cross the bridge, turn left and follow the bank until you reach Huntingdon Cross and the junction with the River Avon. If the weather is good, cross the path to Pupers Hill and then bear left and head SW across open moorland on the shoulder of Hickaton Hill. Drop down to the right of an enclosure to the Western Wella Brook and cross the wall via a stile.

Follow the northern bank of the River Avon upstream to a clapper bridge.

Cross the clapper bridge and either follow the obvious path steeply uphill towards a ruined building on the skyline or follow the indistinct route of the Abbot's Way that contours around the hill to your left for a short distance before turning uphill just before you reach a marshy area.

N

S

Pupers Hill

Huntingdon Warren

Bridge

Tin mine

Blowing House

Vermin Trap

Huntingdon Barrow or Heap of Sinners

Warren House

Old Leat

Western Wella Brook

Keble Martin church (ruin)

Hickaton Hill
Enclosed Hut Group

Enclosed Hut Groups

Huntingdon Cross

Ford

Enclosure & Hut Circles

Clapper Bridge

Ring Cairn

River Avon

Bishop's Meads

Abbot's Way

Huntingdon Cross is known to have been standing in 1557.

Abbot's Way

Alternative Route ● ● ● ● ● ● ● ●

The Abbot's Way, followed for only about 1km, is reputed to have linked Buckfast Abbey with the Abbeys of Tavistock and Buckland Monachorum, though it is much more likely to have been purely a jobbers' path and may well have been used even in prehistoric times. Originally it continued eastwards on the southern bank of the River Avon, but it is difficult to ford at Huntingdon Cross and it is wise to use the 19th Century clapper bridge.

In 1909 the Rev. Keble Martin and some friends built a tiny church in the dried out leat just north of a wheel pit. It is now in ruins, but is of interest in view of Keble Martin's subsequent fame as a painter of British wild flowers.

North-bound

From here you can either take the direct route following the path as it drops away to the left, gently at first and then more steeply to reach a clapper bridge across the River Avon. Alternatively, you can follow the Abbot's Way onwards a short distance to a gully and from there more gently downhill to the river.

Cross the Avon and follow its north bank to the wall at Huntingdon Cross. Climb the stile over the wall and ford the Western Wella Brook. (If the Brook is in spate, detour northwards to the bridge near Warren House and then follow the track eastwards across the slope of Pupers Hill.)

Follow the path uphill to the left of the enclosure and on across open moorland passing between the tor on the top of Pupers Hill on your left and the marshy area to your right to find the junction where the path to Huntingdon Warren crosses the path to Pupers Hill. Take the Huntingdon Warren path eastwards (away from the Warren).

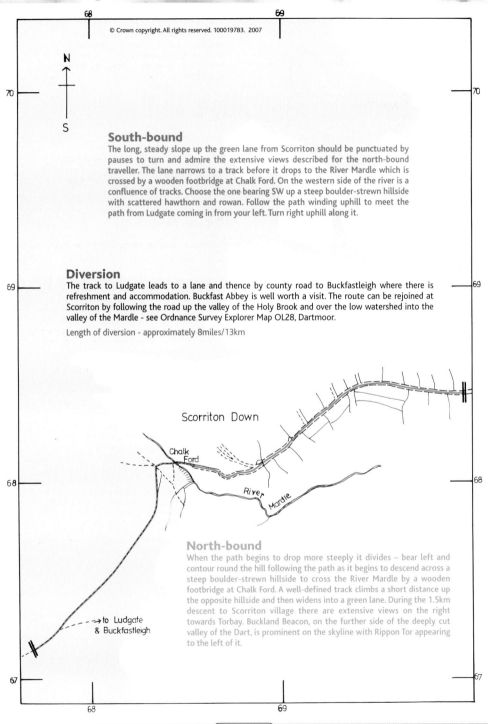

South-bound

The long, steady slope up the green lane from Scorriton should be punctuated by pauses to turn and admire the extensive views described for the north-bound traveller. The lane narrows to a track before it drops to the River Mardle which is crossed by a wooden footbridge at Chalk Ford. On the western side of the river is a confluence of tracks. Choose the one bearing SW up a steep boulder-strewn hillside with scattered hawthorn and rowan. Follow the path winding uphill to meet the path from Ludgate coming in from your left. Turn right uphill along it.

Diversion

The track to Ludgate leads to a lane and thence by county road to Buckfastleigh where there is refreshment and accommodation. Buckfast Abbey is well worth a visit. The route can be rejoined at Scorriton by following the road up the valley of the Holy Brook and over the low watershed into the valley of the Mardle - see Ordnance Survey Explorer Map OL28, Dartmoor.

Length of diversion - approximately 8miles/13km

North-bound

When the path begins to drop more steeply it divides – bear left and contour round the hill following the path as it begins to descend across a steep boulder-strewn hillside to cross the River Mardle by a wooden footbridge at Chalk Ford. A well-defined track climbs a short distance up the opposite hillside and then widens into a green lane. During the 1.5km descent to Scorriton village there are extensive views on the right towards Torbay. Buckland Beacon, on the further side of the deeply cut valley of the Dart, is prominent on the skyline with Rippon Tor appearing to the left of it.

N10 S29

See key to maps on page 7

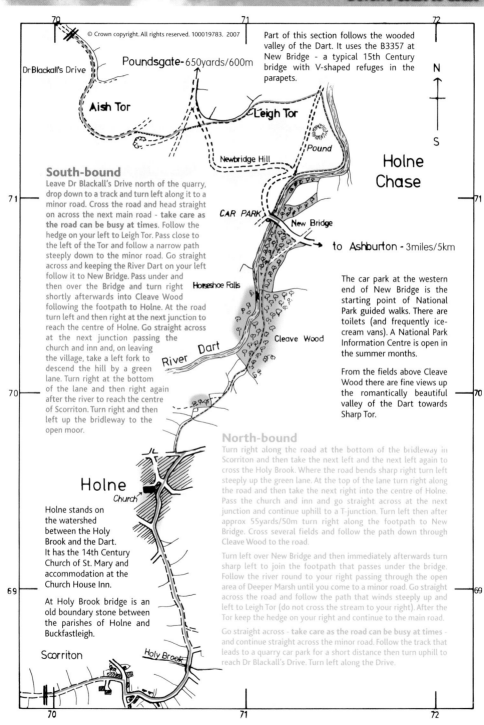

70   71   72

Dr Blackall's Drive

Poundsgate - 650yards/600m

Aish Tor

Leigh Tor

Newbridge Hill

Pound

Part of this section follows the wooded valley of the Dart. It uses the B3357 at New Bridge - a typical 15th Century bridge with V-shaped refuges in the parapets.

N

S

Holne Chase

South-bound

Leave Dr Blackall's Drive north of the quarry, drop down to a track and turn left along it to a minor road. Cross the road and head straight on across the next main road - **take care as the road can be busy at times.** Follow the hedge on your left to Leigh Tor. Pass close to the left of the Tor and follow a narrow path steeply down to the minor road. Go straight across and keeping the River Dart on your left follow it to New Bridge. Pass under and then over the Bridge and turn right shortly afterwards into Cleave Wood following the footpath to Holne. At the road turn left and then right **at the next junction** to reach the centre of Holne. Go straight across at the next junction passing the church and inn and, on leaving the village, take a left fork to descend the hill by a green lane. Turn right at the bottom of the lane and then right again after the river to reach the centre of Scorriton. Turn right and then left up the bridleway to the open moor.

CAR PARK

New Bridge

to Ashburton - 3miles/5km

Horseshoe Falls

Cleave Wood

River Dart

The car park at the western end of New Bridge is the starting point of National Park guided walks. There are toilets (and frequently ice-cream vans). A National Park Information Centre is open in the summer months.

From the fields above Cleave Wood there are fine views up the romantically beautiful valley of the Dart towards Sharp Tor.

North-bound

Turn right along the road at the bottom of the bridleway in Scorriton and then take the next left and the next left again to cross the Holy Brook. Where the road bends sharp right turn left steeply up the green lane. At the top of the lane turn right along the road and then take the next right into the centre of Holne. Pass the church and inn and go straight across at the next junction and continue uphill to a T-junction. Turn left then after approx 55yards/50m turn right along the footpath to New Bridge. Cross several fields and follow the path down through Cleave Wood to the road.

Turn left over New Bridge and then immediately afterwards turn sharp left to join the footpath that passes under the bridge. Follow the river round to your right passing through the open area of Deeper Marsh until you come to a minor road. Go straight across the road and follow the path that winds steeply up and left to Leigh Tor (do not cross the stream to your right). After the Tor keep the hedge on your right and continue to the main road.

Go straight across - **take care as the road can be busy at times** - and continue straight across the minor road. Follow the track that leads to a quarry car park for a short distance then turn uphill to reach Dr Blackall's Drive. Turn left along the Drive.

Holne

Church

Holne stands on the watershed between the Holy Brook and the Dart. It has the 14th Century Church of St. Mary and accommodation at the Church House Inn.

At Holy Brook bridge is an old boundary stone between the parishes of Holne and Buckfastleigh.

Scorriton

Holy Brook

70   71   72

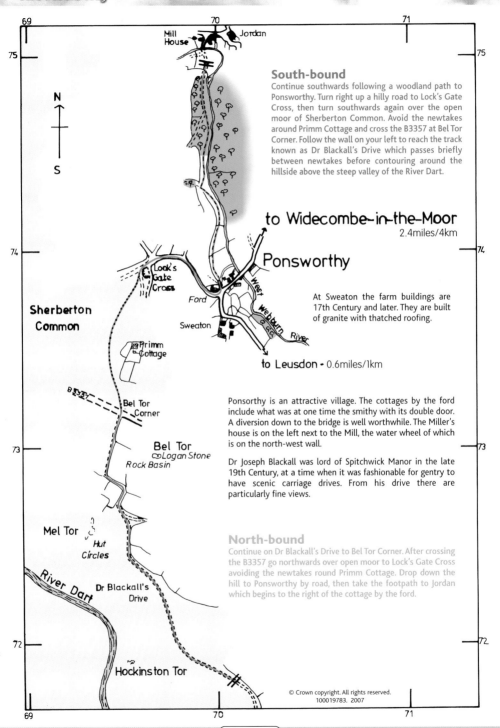

South-bound

Continue southwards following a woodland path to Ponsworthy. Turn right up a hilly road to Lock's Gate Cross, then turn southwards again over the open moor of Sherberton Common. Avoid the newtakes around Primm Cottage and cross the B3357 at Bel Tor Corner. Follow the wall on your left to reach the track known as Dr Blackall's Drive which passes briefly between newtakes before contouring around the hillside above the steep valley of the River Dart.

to Widecombe-in-the-Moor
2.4miles/4km

Ponsworthy

At Sweaton the farm buildings are 17th Century and later. They are built of granite with thatched roofing.

to Leusdon - 0.6miles/1km

Ponsworthy is an attractive village. The cottages by the ford include what was at one time the smithy with its double door. A diversion down to the bridge is well worthwhile. The Miller's house is on the left next to the Mill, the water wheel of which is on the north-west wall.

Dr Joseph Blackall was lord of Spitchwick Manor in the late 19th Century, at a time when it was fashionable for gentry to have scenic carriage drives. From his drive there are particularly fine views.

North-bound

Continue on Dr Blackall's Drive to Bel Tor Corner. After crossing the B3357 go northwards over open moor to Lock's Gate Cross avoiding the newtakes round Primm Cottage. Drop down the hill to Ponsworthy by road, then take the footpath to Jordan which begins to the right of the cottage by the ford.

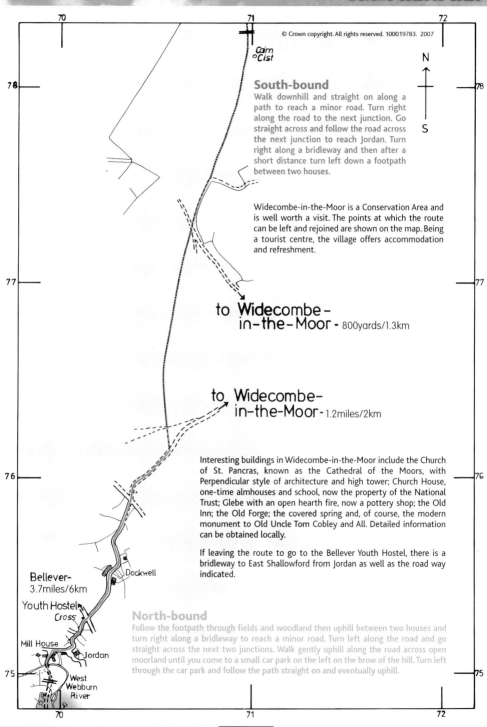

Cairn
Cist

N

S

South-bound

Walk downhill and straight on along a path to reach a minor road. Turn right along the road to the next junction. Go straight across and follow the road across the next junction to reach Jordan. Turn right along a bridleway and then after a short distance turn left down a footpath between two houses.

Widecombe-in-the-Moor is a Conservation Area and is well worth a visit. The points at which the route can be left and rejoined are shown on the map. Being a tourist centre, the village offers accommodation and refreshment.

to Widecombe-in-the-Moor - 800yards/1.3km

to Widecombe-in-the-Moor - 1.2miles/2km

Interesting buildings in Widecombe-in-the-Moor include the Church of St. Pancras, known as the Cathedral of the Moors, with Perpendicular style of architecture and high tower; Church House, one-time almhouses and school, now the property of the National Trust; Glebe with an open hearth fire, now a pottery shop; the Old Inn; the Old Forge; the covered spring and, of course, the modern monument to Old Uncle Tom Cobley and All. Detailed information can be obtained locally.

If leaving the route to go to the Bellever Youth Hostel, there is a bridleway to East Shallowford from Jordan as well as the road way indicated.

Dockwell

Bellever-
3.7miles/6km

Youth Hostel
Cross

Mill House

Jordan

West
Webburn
River

North-bound

Follow the footpath through fields and woodland then uphill between two houses and turn right along a bridleway to reach a minor road. Turn left along the road and go straight across the next two junctions. Walk gently uphill along the road across open moorland until you come to a small car park on the left on the brow of the hill. Turn left through the car park and follow the path straight on and eventually uphill.

Bridges

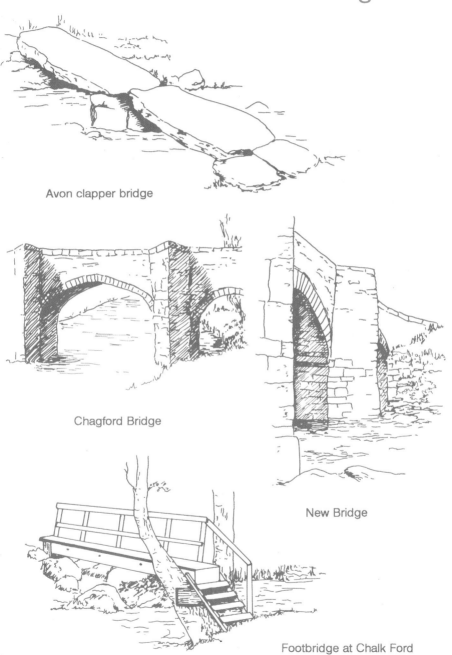

Avon clapper bridge

Chagford Bridge

New Bridge

Footbridge at Chalk Ford

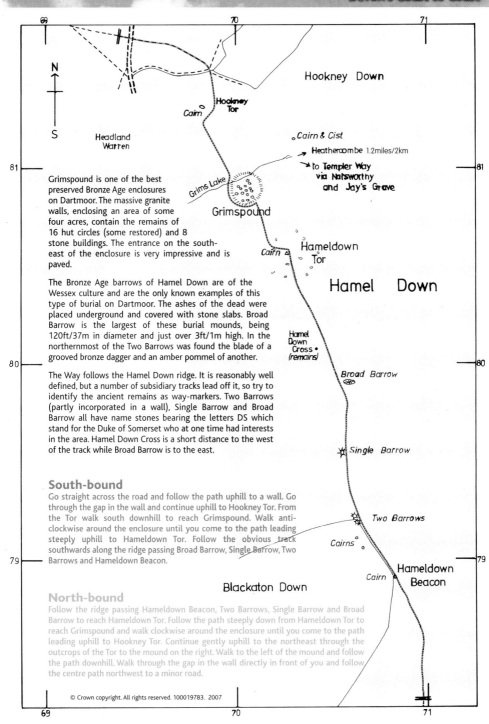

Grimspound is one of the best preserved Bronze Age enclosures on Dartmoor. The massive granite walls, enclosing an area of some four acres, contain the remains of 16 hut circles (some restored) and 8 stone buildings. The entrance on the south-east of the enclosure is very impressive and is paved.

The Bronze Age barrows of Hamel Down are of the Wessex culture and are the only known examples of this type of burial on Dartmoor. The ashes of the dead were placed underground and covered with stone slabs. Broad Barrow is the largest of these burial mounds, being 120ft/37m in diameter and just over 3ft/1m high. In the northernmost of the Two Barrows was found the blade of a grooved bronze dagger and an amber pommel of another.

The Way follows the Hamel Down ridge. It is reasonably well defined, but a number of subsidiary tracks lead off it, so try to identify the ancient remains as way-markers. Two Barrows (partly incorporated in a wall), Single Barrow and Broad Barrow all have name stones bearing the letters DS which stand for the Duke of Somerset who at one time had interests in the area. Hamel Down Cross is a short distance to the west of the track while Broad Barrow is to the east.

South-bound

Go straight across the road and follow the path uphill to a wall. Go through the gap in the wall and continue uphill to Hookney Tor. From the Tor walk south downhill to reach Grimspound. Walk anti-clockwise around the enclosure until you come to the path leading steeply uphill to Hameldown Tor. Follow the obvious track southwards along the ridge passing Broad Barrow, Single Barrow, Two Barrows and Hameldown Beacon.

North-bound

Follow the ridge passing Hameldown Beacon, Two Barrows, Single Barrow and Broad Barrow to reach Hameldown Tor. Follow the path steeply down from Hameldown Tor to reach Grimspound and walk clockwise around the enclosure until you come to the path leading uphill to Hookney Tor. Continue gently uphill to the northeast through the outcrops of the Tor to the mound on the right. Walk to the left of the mound and follow the path downhill. Walk through the gap in the wall directly in front of you and follow the centre path northwest to a minor road.

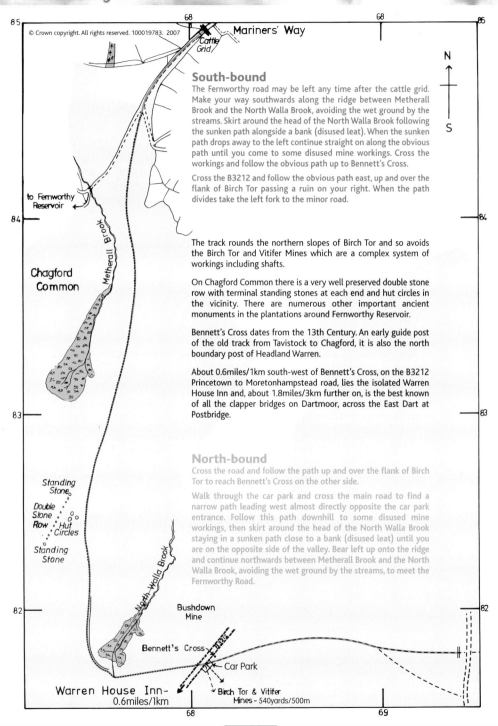

Mariners' Way

N ↑ S

South-bound

The Fernworthy road may be left any time after the cattle grid. Make your way southwards along the ridge between Metherall Brook and the North Walla Brook, avoiding the wet ground by the streams. Skirt around the head of the North Walla Brook following the sunken path alongside a bank (disused leat). When the sunken path drops away to the left continue straight on along the obvious path until you come to some disused mine workings. Cross the workings and follow the obvious path up to Bennett's Cross.

Cross the B3212 and follow the obvious path east, up and over the flank of Birch Tor passing a ruin on your right. When the path divides take the left fork to the minor road.

The track rounds the northern slopes of Birch Tor and so avoids the Birch Tor and Vitifer Mines which are a complex system of workings including shafts.

On Chagford Common there is a very well preserved double stone row with terminal standing stones at each end and hut circles in the vicinity. There are numerous other important ancient monuments in the plantations around Fernworthy Reservoir.

Bennett's Cross dates from the 13th Century. An early guide post of the old track from Tavistock to Chagford, it is also the north boundary post of Headland Warren.

About 0.6miles/1km south-west of Bennett's Cross, on the B3212 Princetown to Moretonhampstead road, lies the isolated Warren House Inn and, about 1.8miles/3km further on, is the best known of all the clapper bridges on Dartmoor, across the East Dart at Postbridge.

North-bound

Cross the road and follow the path up and over the flank of Birch Tor to reach Bennett's Cross on the other side.

Walk through the car park and cross the main road to find a narrow path leading west almost directly opposite the car park entrance. Follow this path downhill to some disused mine workings, then skirt around the head of the North Walla Brook staying in a sunken path close to a bank (disused leat) until you are on the opposite side of the valley. Bear left up onto the ridge and continue northwards between Metherall Brook and the North Walla Brook, avoiding the wet ground by the streams, to meet the Fernworthy Road.

Map labels:
- Cattle Grid
- to Fernworthy Reservoir
- Metherall Brook
- Chagford Common
- Standing Stone
- Double Stone Row
- Hut Circles
- Standing Stone
- North Walla Brook
- Bushdown Mine
- Bennett's Cross
- Car Park
- Warren House Inn — 0.6miles/1km
- Birch Tor & Vitifer Mines – 540yards/500m

N15 S24

See key to maps on page 7

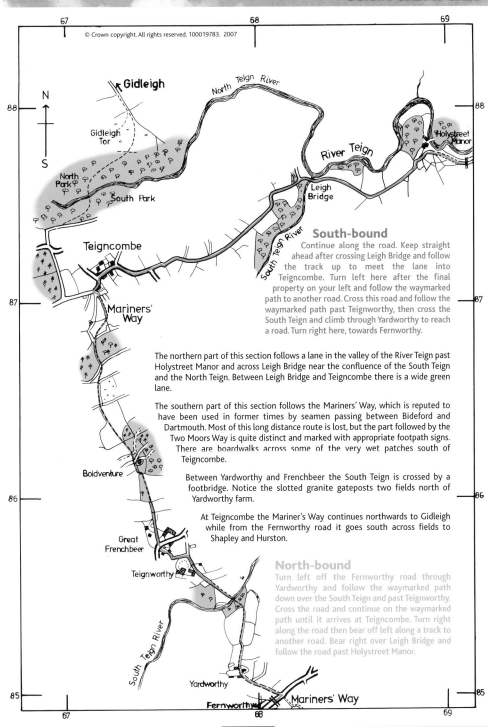

South-bound

Continue along the road. Keep straight ahead after crossing Leigh Bridge and follow the track up to meet the lane into Teigncombe. Turn left here after the final property on your left and follow the waymarked path to another road. Cross this road and follow the waymarked path past Teignworthy, then cross the South Teign and climb through Yardworthy to reach a road. Turn right here, towards Fernworthy.

The northern part of this section follows a lane in the valley of the River Teign past Holystreet Manor and across Leigh Bridge near the confluence of the South Teign and the North Teign. Between Leigh Bridge and Teigncombe there is a wide green lane.

The southern part of this section follows the Mariners' Way, which is reputed to have been used in former times by seamen passing between Bideford and Dartmouth. Most of this long distance route is lost, but the part followed by the Two Moors Way is quite distinct and marked with appropriate footpath signs. There are boardwalks across some of the very wet patches south of Teigncombe.

Between Yardworthy and Frenchbeer the South Teign is crossed by a footbridge. Notice the slotted granite gateposts two fields north of Yardworthy farm.

At Teigncombe the Mariner's Way continues northwards to Gidleigh while from the Fernworthy road it goes south across fields to Shapley and Hurston.

North-bound

Turn left off the Fernworthy road through Yardworthy and follow the waymarked path down over the South Teign and past Teignworthy. Cross the road and continue on the waymarked path until it arrives at Teigncombe. Turn right along the road then bear off left along a track to another road. Bear right over Leigh Bridge and follow the road past Holystreet Manor.

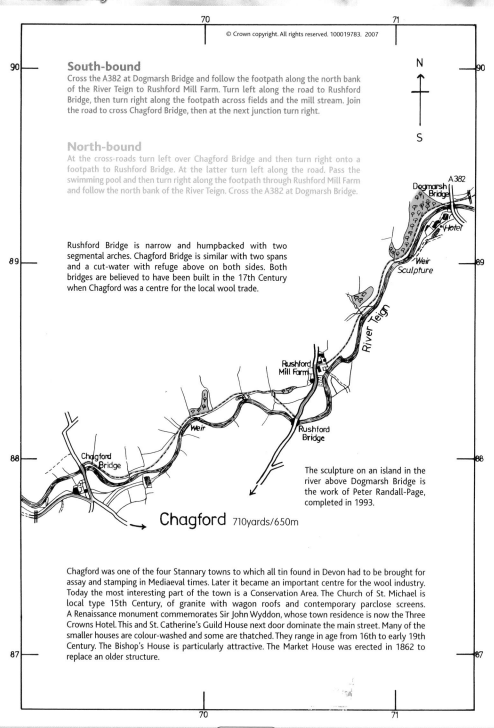

South-bound

Cross the A382 at Dogmarsh Bridge and follow the footpath along the north bank of the River Teign to Rushford Mill Farm. Turn left along the road to Rushford Bridge, then turn right along the footpath across fields and the mill stream. Join the road to cross Chagford Bridge, then at the next junction turn right.

North-bound

At the cross-roads turn left over Chagford Bridge and then turn right onto a footpath to Rushford Bridge. At the latter turn left along the road. Pass the swimming pool and then turn right along the footpath through Rushford Mill Farm and follow the north bank of the River Teign. Cross the A382 at Dogmarsh Bridge.

Rushford Bridge is narrow and humpbacked with two segmental arches. Chagford Bridge is similar with two spans and a cut-water with refuge above on both sides. Both bridges are believed to have been built in the 17th Century when Chagford was a centre for the local wool trade.

Chagford 710yards/650m

The sculpture on an island in the river above Dogmarsh Bridge is the work of Peter Randall-Page, completed in 1993.

Chagford was one of the four Stannary towns to which all tin found in Devon had to be brought for assay and stamping in Mediaeval times. Later it became an important centre for the wool industry. Today the most interesting part of the town is a Conservation Area. The Church of St. Michael is local type 15th Century, of granite with wagon roofs and contemporary parclose screens. A Renaissance monument commemorates Sir John Wyddon, whose town residence is now the Three Crowns Hotel. This and St. Catherine's Guild House next door dominate the main street. Many of the smaller houses are colour-washed and some are thatched. They range in age from 16th to early 19th Century. The Bishop's House is particularly attractive. The Market House was erected in 1862 to replace an older structure.

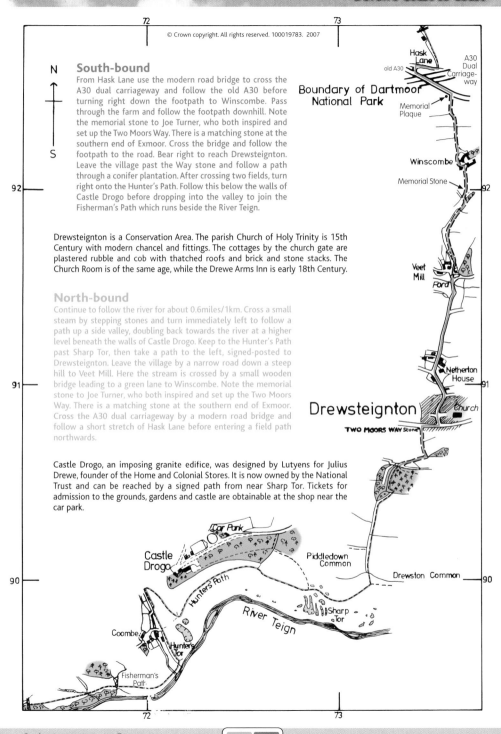

South-bound

From Hask Lane use the modern road bridge to cross the A30 dual carriageway and follow the old A30 before turning right down the footpath to Winscombe. Pass through the farm and follow the footpath downhill. Note the memorial stone to Joe Turner, who both inspired and set up the Two Moors Way. There is a matching stone at the southern end of Exmoor. Cross the bridge and follow the footpath to the road. Bear right to reach Drewsteignton. Leave the village past the Way stone and follow a path through a conifer plantation. After crossing two fields, turn right onto the Hunter's Path. Follow this below the walls of Castle Drogo before dropping into the valley to join the Fisherman's Path which runs beside the River Teign.

Drewsteignton is a Conservation Area. The parish Church of Holy Trinity is 15th Century with modern chancel and fittings. The cottages by the church gate are plastered rubble and cob with thatched roofs and brick and stone stacks. The Church Room is of the same age, while the Drewe Arms Inn is early 18th Century.

North-bound

Continue to follow the river for about 0.6miles/1km. Cross a small steam by stepping stones and turn immediately left to follow a path up a side valley, doubling back towards the river at a higher level beneath the walls of Castle Drogo. Keep to the Hunter's Path past Sharp Tor, then take a path to the left, signed-posted to Drewsteignton. Leave the village by a narrow road down a steep hill to Veet Mill. Here the stream is crossed by a small wooden bridge leading to a green lane to Winscombe. Note the memorial stone to Joe Turner, who both inspired and set up the Two Moors Way. There is a matching stone at the southern end of Exmoor. Cross the A30 dual carriageway by a modern road bridge and follow a short stretch of Hask Lane before entering a field path northwards.

Castle Drogo, an imposing granite edifice, was designed by Lutyens for Julius Drewe, founder of the Home and Colonial Stores. It is now owned by the National Trust and can be reached by a signed path from near Sharp Tor. Tickets for admission to the grounds, gardens and castle are obtainable at the shop near the car park.

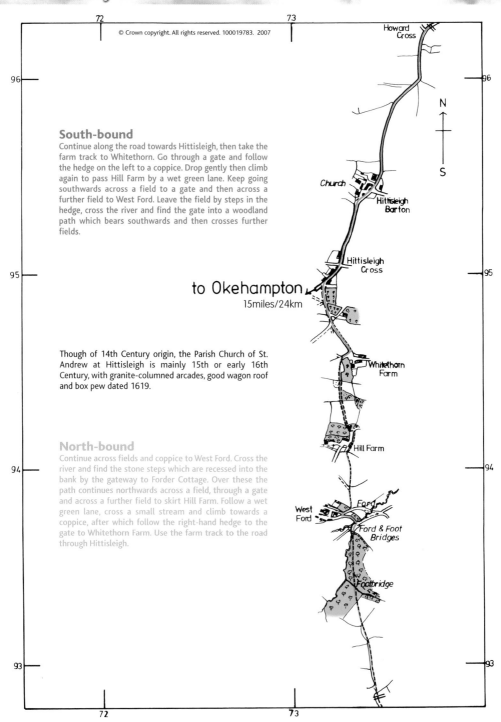

Howard Cross

N

S

South-bound

Continue along the road towards Hittisleigh, then take the farm track to Whitethorn. Go through a gate and follow the hedge on the left to a coppice. Drop gently then climb again to pass Hill Farm by a wet green lane. Keep going southwards across a field to a gate and then across a further field to West Ford. Leave the field by steps in the hedge, cross the river and find the gate into a woodland path which bears southwards and then crosses further fields.

Church

Hittisleigh Barton

Hittisleigh Cross

to Okehampton
15miles/24km

Whitethorn Farm

Though of 14th Century origin, the Parish Church of St. Andrew at Hittisleigh is mainly 15th or early 16th Century, with granite-columned arcades, good wagon roof and box pew dated 1619.

Hill Farm

North-bound

Continue across fields and coppice to West Ford. Cross the river and find the stone steps which are recessed into the bank by the gateway to Forder Cottage. Over these the path continues northwards across a field, through a gate and across a further field to skirt Hill Farm. Follow a wet green lane, cross a small stream and climb towards a coppice, after which follow the right-hand hedge to the gate to Whitethorn Farm. Use the farm track to the road through Hittisleigh.

West Ford

Ford

Ford & Foot Bridges

Footbridge

N19 S20

See key to maps on page 7

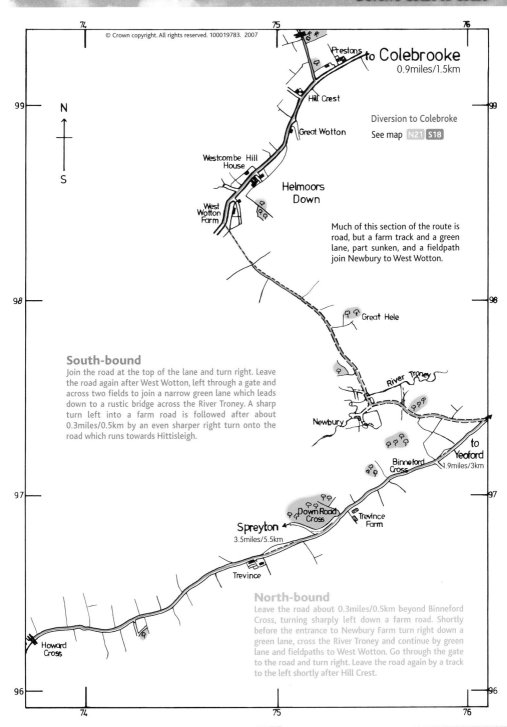

Prestons

to **Colebrooke**
0.9miles/1.5km

Hill Crest

Diversion to Colebroke

See map N21 S18

Great Wotton

N

S

Westcombe Hill House

Helmoors Down

West Wotton Farm

Much of this section of the route is road, but a farm track and a green lane, part sunken, and a fieldpath join Newbury to West Wotton.

Great Hele

South-bound

Join the road at the top of the lane and turn right. Leave the road again after West Wotton, left through a gate and across two fields to join a narrow green lane which leads down to a rustic bridge across the River Troney. A sharp turn left into a farm road is followed after about 0.3miles/0.5km by an even sharper right turn onto the road which runs towards Hittisleigh.

River Troney

Newbury

to **Yeoford**
1.9miles/3km

Binneford Cross

Down Road Cross

Trevince Farm

Spreyton
3.5miles/5.5km

Trevince

North-bound

Leave the road about 0.3miles/0.5km beyond Binneford Cross, turning sharply left down a farm road. Shortly before the entrance to Newbury Farm turn right down a green lane, cross the River Troney and continue by green lane and fieldpaths to West Wotton. Go through the gate to the road and turn right. Leave the road again by a track to the left shortly after Hill Crest.

Howard Cross

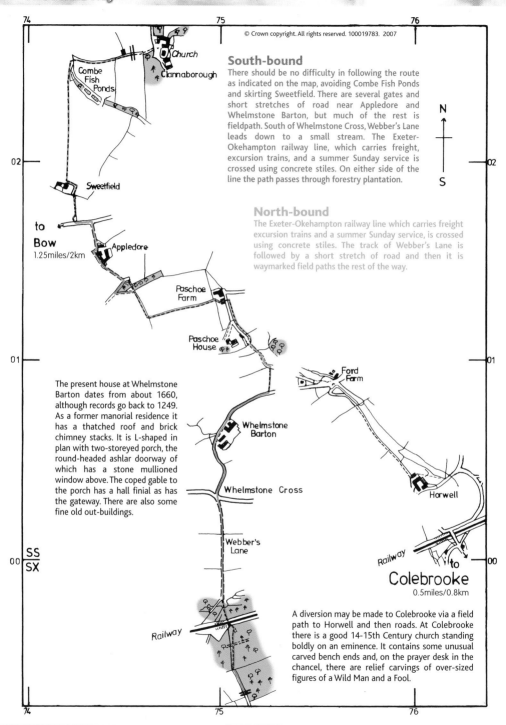

South-bound

There should be no difficulty in following the route as indicated on the map, avoiding Combe Fish Ponds and skirting Sweetfield. There are several gates and short stretches of road near Appledore and Whelmstone Barton, but much of the rest is fieldpath. South of Whelmstone Cross, Webber's Lane leads down to a small stream. The Exeter-Okehampton railway line, which carries freight, excursion trains, and a summer Sunday service is crossed using concrete stiles. On either side of the line the path passes through forestry plantation.

North-bound

The Exeter-Okehampton railway line which carries freight excursion trains and a summer Sunday service, is crossed using concrete stiles. The track of Webber's Lane is followed by a short stretch of road and then it is waymarked field paths the rest of the way.

The present house at Whelmstone Barton dates from about 1660, although records go back to 1249. As a former manorial residence it has a thatched roof and brick chimney stacks. It is L-shaped in plan with two-storeyed porch, the round-headed ashlar doorway of which has a stone mullioned window above. The coped gable to the porch has a hall finial as has the gateway. There are also some fine old out-buildings.

A diversion may be made to Colebrooke via a field path to Horwell and then roads. At Colebrooke there is a good 14-15th Century church standing boldly on an eminence. It contains some unusual carved bench ends and, on the prayer desk in the chancel, there are relief carvings of over-sized figures of a Wild Man and a Fool.

Churches

Holy Trinity Church
- Drewsteignton

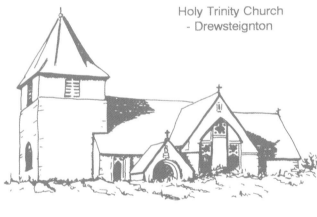

Church of St Peter
-Washford Pyne

Font in the Church of St Andrew
- Hittisleigh

Church of St Mary
- Morchard Bishop

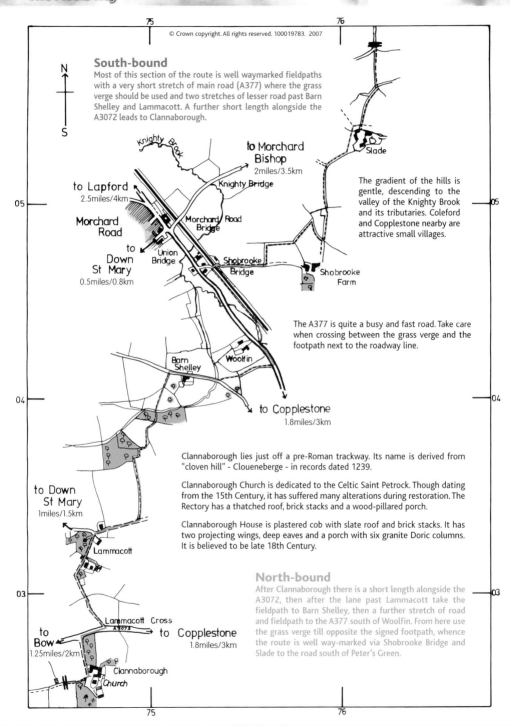

South-bound

Most of this section of the route is well waymarked fieldpaths with a very short stretch of main road (A377) where the grass verge should be used and two stretches of lesser road past Barn Shelley and Lammacott. A further short length alongside the A3072 leads to Clannaborough.

The gradient of the hills is gentle, descending to the valley of the Knighty Brook and its tributaries. Coleford and Copplestone nearby are attractive small villages.

The A377 is quite a busy and fast road. Take care when crossing between the grass verge and the footpath next to the roadway line.

Clannaborough lies just off a pre-Roman trackway. Its name is derived from "cloven hill" - Cloueneberge - in records dated 1239.

Clannaborough Church is dedicated to the Celtic Saint Petrock. Though dating from the 15th Century, it has suffered many alterations during restoration. The Rectory has a thatched roof, brick stacks and a wood-pillared porch.

Clannaborough House is plastered cob with slate roof and brick stacks. It has two projecting wings, deep eaves and a porch with six granite Doric columns. It is believed to be late 18th Century.

North-bound

After Clannaborough there is a short length alongside the A3072, then after the lane past Lammacott take the fieldpath to Barn Shelley, then a further stretch of road and fieldpath to the A377 south of Woolfin. From here use the grass verge till opposite the signed footpath, whence the route is well way-marked via Shobrooke Bridge and Slade to the road south of Peter's Green.

Map labels:
- to Morchard Bishop 2miles/3.5km
- Knighty Brook
- Knighty Bridge
- Slade
- to Lapford 2.5miles/4km
- Morchard Road
- Morchard Road Bridge
- to Down St Mary 0.5miles/0.8km
- Union Bridge
- Shobrooke Bridge
- Shobrooke Farm
- Barn Shelley
- Woolfin
- to Copplestone 1.8miles/3km
- to Down St Mary 1miles/1.5km
- Lammacott
- Lammacott Cross
- A3072
- to Bow 1.25miles/2km
- to Copplestone 1.8miles/3km
- Clannaborough Church

N22 S17

See key to maps on page 7

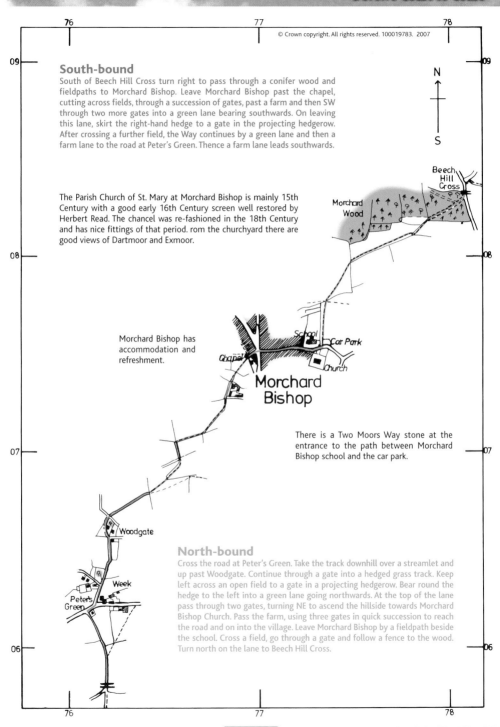

© Crown copyright. All rights reserved. 100019783. 2007

South-bound

South of Beech Hill Cross turn right to pass through a conifer wood and fieldpaths to Morchard Bishop. Leave Morchard Bishop past the chapel, cutting across fields, through a succession of gates, past a farm and then SW through two more gates into a green lane bearing southwards. On leaving this lane, skirt the right-hand hedge to a gate in the projecting hedgerow. After crossing a further field, the Way continues by a green lane and then a farm lane to the road at Peter's Green. Thence a farm lane leads southwards.

The Parish Church of St. Mary at Morchard Bishop is mainly 15th Century with a good early 16th Century screen well restored by Herbert Read. The chancel was re-fashioned in the 18th Century and has nice fittings of that period. rom the churchyard there are good views of Dartmoor and Exmoor.

Morchard Bishop has accommodation and refreshment.

There is a Two Moors Way stone at the entrance to the path between Morchard Bishop school and the car park.

North-bound

Cross the road at Peter's Green. Take the track downhill over a streamlet and up past Woodgate. Continue through a gate into a hedged grass track. Keep left across an open field to a gate in a projecting hedgerow. Bear round the hedge to the left into a green lane going northwards. At the top of the lane pass through two gates, turning NE to ascend the hillside towards Morchard Bishop Church. Pass the farm, using three gates in quick succession to reach the road and on into the village. Leave Morchard Bishop by a fieldpath beside the school. Cross a field, go through a gate and follow a fence to the wood. Turn north on the lane to Beech Hill Cross.

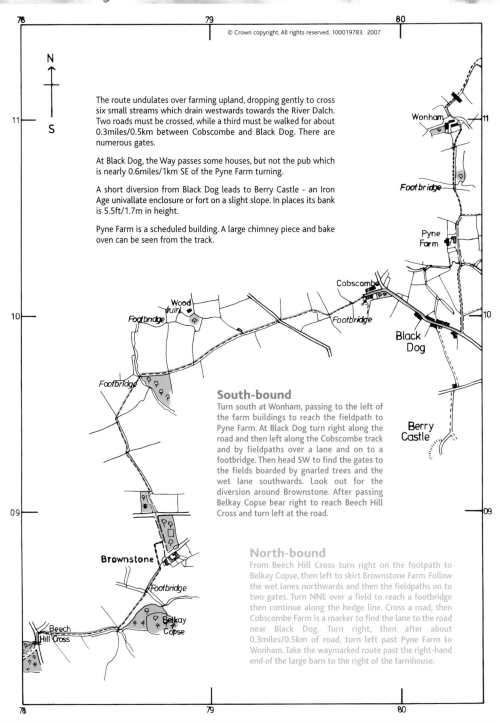

The route undulates over farming upland, dropping gently to cross six small streams which drain westwards towards the River Dalch. Two roads must be crossed, while a third must be walked for about 0.3miles/0.5km between Cobscombe and Black Dog. There are numerous gates.

At Black Dog, the Way passes some houses, but not the pub which is nearly 0.6miles/1km SE of the Pyne Farm turning.

A short diversion from Black Dog leads to Berry Castle - an Iron Age univallate enclosure or fort on a slight slope. In places its bank is 5.5ft/1.7m in height.

Pyne Farm is a scheduled building. A large chimney piece and bake oven can be seen from the track.

South-bound

Turn south at Wonham, passing to the left of the farm buildings to reach the fieldpath to Pyne Farm. At Black Dog turn right along the road and then left along the Cobscombe track and by fieldpaths over a lane and on to a footbridge. Then head SW to find the gates to the fields boarded by gnarled trees and the wet lane southwards. Look out for the diversion around Brownstone. After passing Belkay Copse bear right to reach Beech Hill Cross and turn left at the road.

North-bound

From Beech Hill Cross turn right on the footpath to Belkay Copse, then left to skirt Brownstone Farm. Follow the wet lanes northwards and then the fieldpaths on to two gates. Turn NNE over a field to reach a footbridge then continue along the hedge line. Cross a road, then Cobscombe Farm is a marker to find the lane to the road near Black Dog. Turn right, then after about 0.3miles/0.5km of road, turn left past Pyne Farm to Wonham. Take the waymarked route past the right-hand end of the large barn to the right of the farmhouse.

N24 S15

See key to maps on page 7

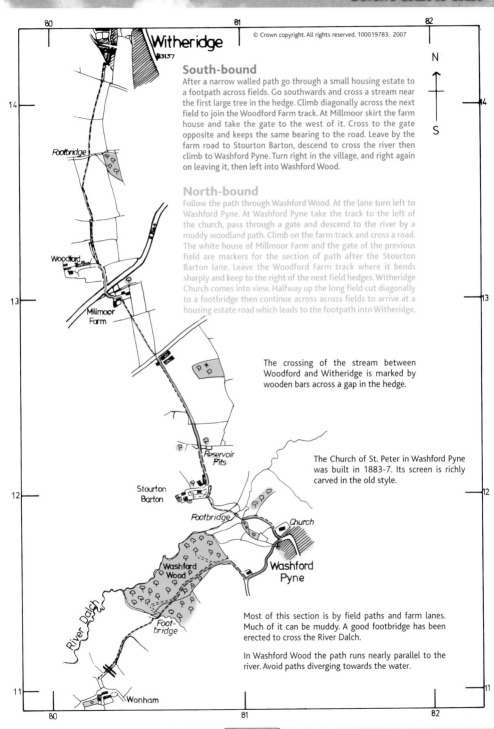

Witheridge
B3137

N
↑
+
S

South-bound

After a narrow walled path go through a small housing estate to a footpath across fields. Go southwards and cross a stream near the first large tree in the hedge. Climb diagonally across the next field to join the Woodford Farm track. At Millmoor skirt the farm house and take the gate to the west of it. Cross to the gate opposite and keeps the same bearing to the road. Leave by the farm road to Stourton Barton, descend to cross the river then climb to Washford Pyne. Turn right in the village, and right again on leaving it, then left into Washford Wood.

North-bound

Follow the path through Washford Wood. At the lane turn left to Washford Pyne. At Washford Pyne take the track to the left of the church, pass through a gate and descend to the river by a muddy woodland path. Climb on the farm track and cross a road. The white house of Millmoor Farm and the gate of the previous field are markers for the section of path after the Stourton Barton lane. Leave the Woodford Farm track where it bends sharply and keep to the right of the next field hedges. Witheridge Church comes into view. Halfway up the long field cut diagonally to a footbridge then continue across across fields to arrive at a housing estate road which leads to the footpath into Witheridge.

The crossing of the stream between Woodford and Witheridge is marked by wooden bars across a gap in the hedge.

The Church of St. Peter in Washford Pyne was built in 1883-7. Its screen is richly carved in the old style.

Most of this section is by field paths and farm lanes. Much of it can be muddy. A good footbridge has been erected to cross the River Dalch.

In Washford Wood the path runs nearly parallel to the river. Avoid paths diverging towards the water.

Map labels: Footbridge, Woodford, Millmoor Farm, Reservoir Pits, Stourton Barton, Footbridge, Church, Washford Wood, Washford Pyne, Foot-bridge, River Dalch, Wonham

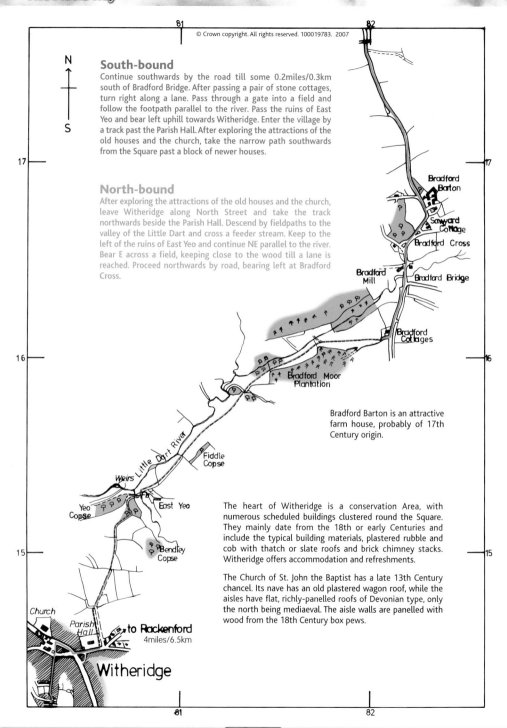

South-bound

Continue southwards by the road till some 0.2miles/0.3km south of Bradford Bridge. After passing a pair of stone cottages, turn right along a lane. Pass through a gate into a field and follow the footpath parallel to the river. Pass the ruins of East Yeo and bear left uphill towards Witheridge. Enter the village by a track past the Parish Hall. After exploring the attractions of the old houses and the church, take the narrow path southwards from the Square past a block of newer houses.

North-bound

After exploring the attractions of the old houses and the church, leave Witheridge along North Street and take the track northwards beside the Parish Hall. Descend by fieldpaths to the valley of the Little Dart and cross a feeder stream. Keep to the left of the ruins of East Yeo and continue NE parallel to the river. Bear E across a field, keeping close to the wood till a lane is reached. Proceed northwards by road, bearing left at Bradford Cross.

Bradford Barton is an attractive farm house, probably of 17th Century origin.

The heart of Witheridge is a conservation Area, with numerous scheduled buildings clustered round the Square. They mainly date from the 18th or early Centuries and include the typical building materials, plastered rubble and cob with thatch or slate roofs and brick chimney stacks. Witheridge offers accommodation and refreshments.

The Church of St. John the Baptist has a late 13th Century chancel. Its nave has an old plastered wagon roof, while the aisles have flat, richly-panelled roofs of Devonian type, only the north being mediaeval. The aisle walls are panelled with wood from the 18th Century box pews.

to Rockenford
4miles/6.5km

Witheridge

N26 S13

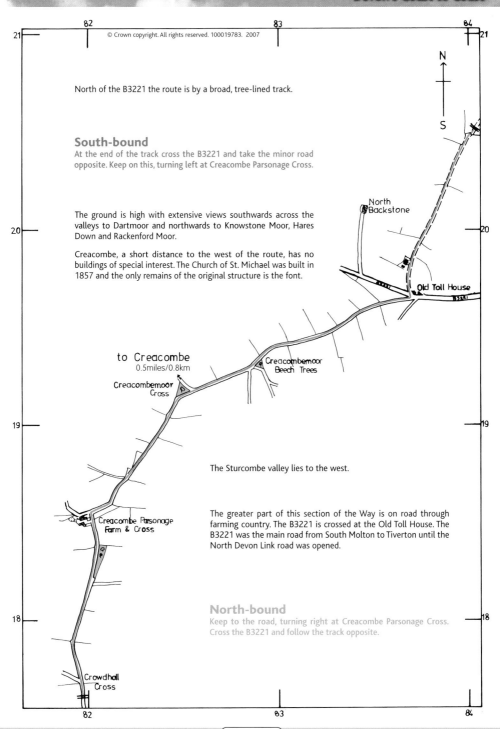

North of the B3221 the route is by a broad, tree-lined track.

South-bound

At the end of the track cross the B3221 and take the minor road opposite. Keep on this, turning left at Creacombe Parsonage Cross.

The ground is high with extensive views southwards across the valleys to Dartmoor and northwards to Knowstone Moor, Hares Down and Rackenford Moor.

Creacombe, a short distance to the west of the route, has no buildings of special interest. The Church of St. Michael was built in 1857 and the only remains of the original structure is the font.

North
Backstone

Old Toll House

to Creacombe
0.5miles/0.8km

Creacombemoor
Beech Trees

Creacombemoor
Cross

The Sturcombe valley lies to the west.

The greater part of this section of the Way is on road through farming country. The B3221 is crossed at the Old Toll House. The B3221 was the main road from South Molton to Tiverton until the North Devon Link road was opened.

Creacombe Parsonage
Farm & Cross

North-bound

Keep to the road, turning right at Creacombe Parsonage Cross. Cross the B3221 and follow the track opposite.

Crowdhall
Cross

Wayside Inns

Church House Inn
- Holne

Drewe Arms
- Drewsteignton

Abandoned
cider press

Mason's Arms
- Knowstone

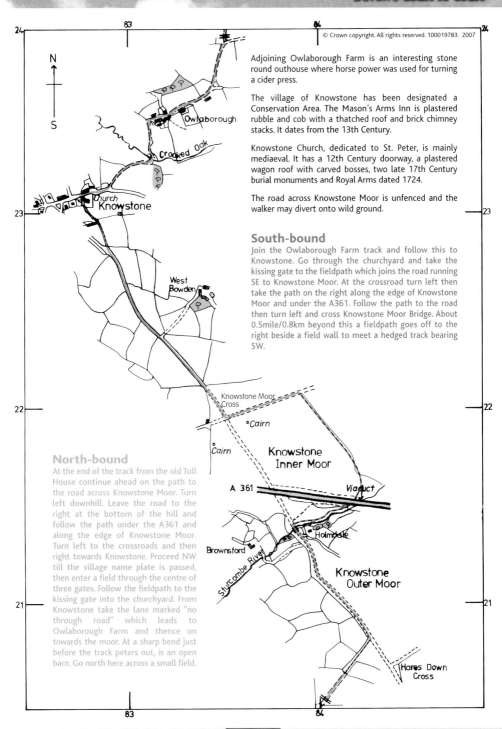

N
↑
S

Adjoining Owlaborough Farm is an interesting stone round outhouse where horse power was used for turning a cider press.

The village of Knowstone has been designated a Conservation Area. The Mason's Arms Inn is plastered rubble and cob with a thatched roof and brick chimney stacks. It dates from the 13th Century.

Knowstone Church, dedicated to St. Peter, is mainly mediaeval. It has a 12th Century doorway, a plastered wagon roof with carved bosses, two late 17th Century burial monuments and Royal Arms dated 1724.

The road across Knowstone Moor is unfenced and the walker may divert onto wild ground.

South-bound

Join the Owlaborough Farm track and follow this to Knowstone. Go through the churchyard and take the kissing gate to the fieldpath which joins the road running SE to Knowstone Moor. At the crossroad turn left then take the path on the right along the edge of Knowstone Moor and under the A361. Follow the path to the road then turn left and cross Knowstone Moor Bridge. About 0.5mile/0.8km beyond this a fieldpath goes off to the right beside a field wall to meet a hedged track bearing SW.

North-bound

At the end of the track from the old Toll House continue ahead on the path to the road across Knowstone Moor. Turn left downhill. Leave the road to the right at the bottom of the hill and follow the path under the A361 and along the edge of Knowstone Moor. Turn left to the crossroads and then right towards Knowstone. Proceed NW till the village name plate is passed, then enter a field through the centre of three gates. Follow the fieldpath to the kissing gate into the churchyard. From Knowstone take the lane marked "no through road" which leads to Owlaborough Farm and thence on towards the moor. At a sharp bend just before the track peters out, is an open barn. Go north here across a small field.

Map labels: Owlaborough · Crooked Oak · Church · Knowstone · West Bowden · Knowstone Moor Cross · °Cairn · °Cairn · Knowstone Inner Moor · A 361 · Viaduct · Brownsford · Holmdale · Sturcombe River · Knowstone Outer Moor · Hares Down Cross

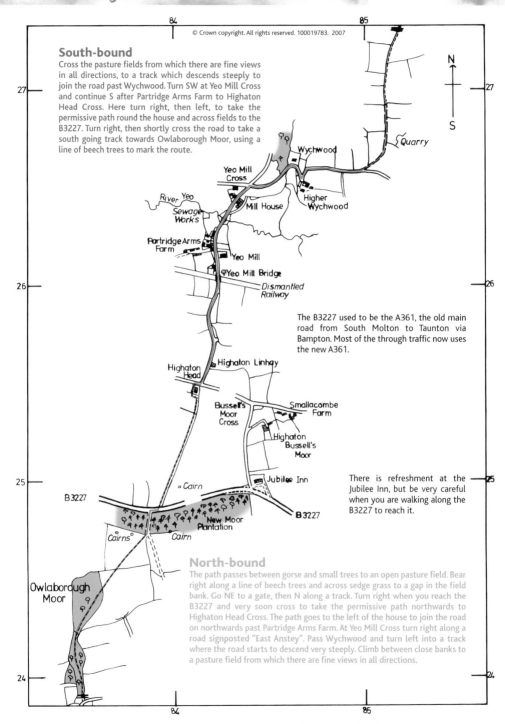

South-bound

Cross the pasture fields from which there are fine views in all directions, to a track which descends steeply to join the road past Wychwood. Turn SW at Yeo Mill Cross and continue S after Partridge Arms Farm to Highaton Head Cross. Here turn right, then left, to take the permissive path round the house and across fields to the B3227. Turn right, then shortly cross the road to take a south going track towards Owlaborough Moor, using a line of beech trees to mark the route.

N
S

Quarry

Wychwood

Yeo Mill Cross

River Yeo

Sewage Works

Mill House

Higher Wychwood

Partridge Arms Farm

Yeo Mill

Yeo Mill Bridge

Dismantled Railway

The B3227 used to be the A361, the old main road from South Molton to Taunton via Bampton. Most of the through traffic now uses the new A361.

Highaton Head

Highaton Linhay

Bussell's Moor Cross

Smallacombe Farm

Highaton Bussell's Moor

Cairn

Jubilee Inn

There is refreshment at the Jubilee Inn, but be very careful when you are walking along the B3227 to reach it.

B3227

B3227

New Moor Plantation

Cairns

Cairn

North-bound

The path passes between gorse and small trees to an open pasture field. Bear right along a line of beech trees and across sedge grass to a gap in the field bank. Go NE to a gate, then N along a track. Turn right when you reach the B3227 and very soon cross to take the permissive path northwards to Highaton Head Cross. The path goes to the left of the house to join the road on northwards past Partridge Arms Farm. At Yeo Mill Cross turn right along a road signposted "East Anstey". Pass Wychwood and turn left into a track where the road starts to descend very steeply. Climb between close banks to a pasture field from which there are fine views in all directions.

Owlaborough Moor

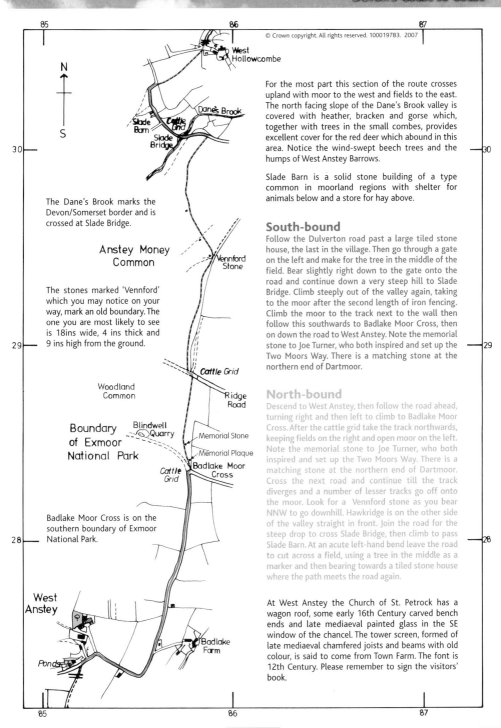

For the most part this section of the route crosses upland to the west and fields to the east. The north facing slope of the Dane's Brook valley is covered with heather, bracken and gorse which, together with trees in the small combes, provides excellent cover for the red deer which abound in this area. Notice the wind-swept beech trees and the humps of West Anstey Barrows.

Slade Barn is a solid stone building of a type common in moorland regions with shelter for animals below and a store for hay above.

South-bound

Follow the Dulverton road past a large tiled stone house, the last in the village. Then go through a gate on the left and make for the tree in the middle of the field. Bear slightly right down to the gate onto the road and continue down a very steep hill to Slade Bridge. Climb steeply out of the valley again, taking to the moor after the second length of iron fencing. Climb the moor to the track next to the wall then follow this southwards to Badlake Moor Cross, then on down the road to West Anstey. Note the memorial stone to Joe Turner, who both inspired and set up the Two Moors Way. There is a matching stone at the northern end of Dartmoor.

North-bound

Descend to West Anstey, then follow the road ahead, turning right and then left to climb to Badlake Moor Cross. After the cattle grid take the track northwards, keeping fields on the right and open moor on the left. Note the memorial stone to Joe Turner, who both inspired and set up the Two Moors Way. There is a matching stone at the northern end of Dartmoor. Cross the next road and continue till the track diverges and a number of lesser tracks go off onto the moor. Look for a Vennford stone as you bear NNW to go downhill. Hawkridge is on the other side of the valley straight in front. Join the road for the steep drop to cross Slade Bridge, then climb to pass Slade Barn. At an acute left-hand bend leave the road to cut across a field, using a tree in the middle as a marker and then bearing towards a tiled stone house where the path meets the road again.

At West Anstey the Church of St. Petrock has a wagon roof, some early 16th Century carved bench ends and late mediaeval painted glass in the SE window of the chancel. The tower screen, formed of late mediaeval chamfered joists and beams with old colour, is said to come from Town Farm. The font is 12th Century. Please remember to sign the visitors' book.

The Dane's Brook marks the Devon/Somerset border and is crossed at Slade Bridge.

The stones marked 'Vennford' which you may notice on your way, mark an old boundary. The one you are most likely to see is 18ins wide, 4 ins thick and 9 ins high from the ground.

Badlake Moor Cross is on the southern boundary of Exmoor National Park.

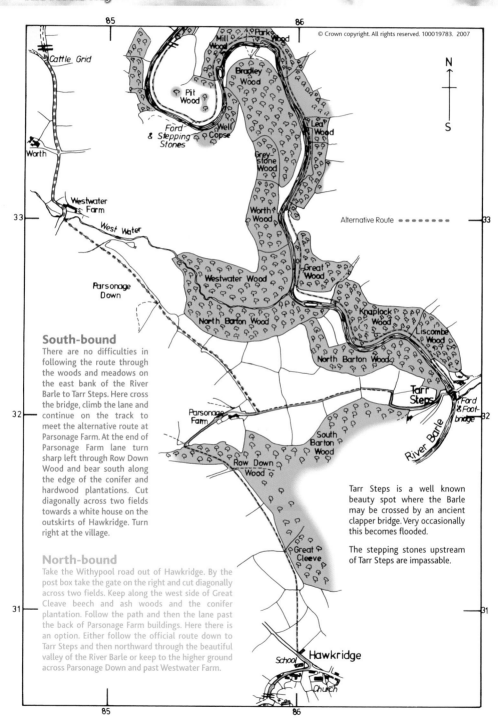

South-bound

There are no difficulties in following the route through the woods and meadows on the east bank of the River Barle to Tarr Steps. Here cross the bridge, climb the lane and continue on the track to meet the alternative route at Parsonage Farm. At the end of Parsonage Farm lane turn sharp left through Row Down Wood and bear south along the edge of the conifer and hardwood plantations. Cut diagonally across two fields towards a white house on the outskirts of Hawkridge. Turn right at the village.

North-bound

Take the Withypool road out of Hawkridge. By the post box take the gate on the right and cut diagonally across two fields. Keep along the west side of Great Cleave beech and ash woods and the conifer plantation. Follow the path and then the lane past the back of Parsonage Farm buildings. Here there is an option. Either follow the official route down to Tarr Steps and then northward through the beautiful valley of the River Barle or keep to the higher ground across Parsonage Down and past Westwater Farm.

Tarr Steps is a well known beauty spot where the Barle may be crossed by an ancient clapper bridge. Very occasionally this becomes flooded.

The stepping stones upstream of Tarr Steps are impassable.

N31 S8

See key to maps on page 7

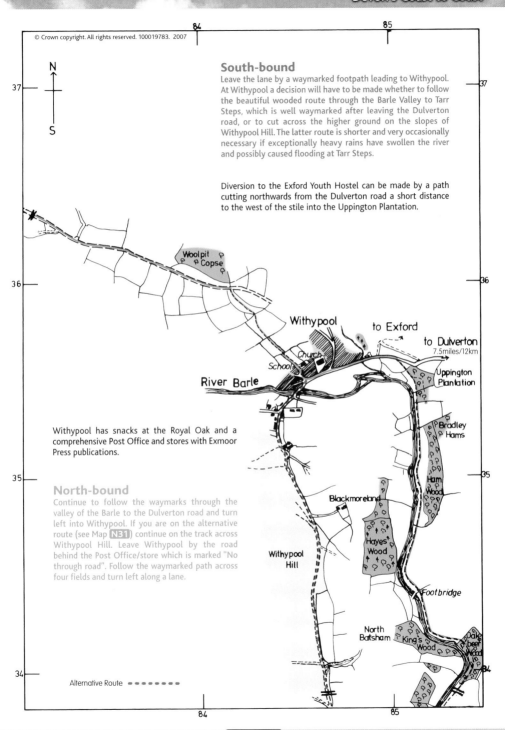

South-bound

Leave the lane by a waymarked footpath leading to Withypool. At Withypool a decision will have to be made whether to follow the beautiful wooded route through the Barle Valley to Tarr Steps, which is well waymarked after leaving the Dulverton road, or to cut across the higher ground on the slopes of Withypool Hill. The latter route is shorter and very occasionally necessary if exceptionally heavy rains have swollen the river and possibly caused flooding at Tarr Steps.

Diversion to the Exford Youth Hostel can be made by a path cutting northwards from the Dulverton road a short distance to the west of the stile into the Uppington Plantation.

Withypool has snacks at the Royal Oak and a comprehensive Post Office and stores with Exmoor Press publications.

North-bound

Continue to follow the waymarks through the valley of the Barle to the Dulverton road and turn left into Withypool. If you are on the alternative route (see Map **N31**) continue on the track across Withypool Hill. Leave Withypool by the road behind the Post Office/store which is marked "No through road". Follow the waymarked path across four fields and turn left along a lane.

Alternative Route ▪ ▪ ▪ ▪ ▪ ▪ ▪ ▪

Map labels: Woolpit Copse, Withypool, to Exford, to Dulverton 7.5miles/12km, Church, School, River Barle, Uppington Plantation, Bradley Hams, Ham Wood, Blackmoreland, Hayes Wood, Withypool Hill, Footbridge, North Batsham, King's Wood, Oaks beer Wood

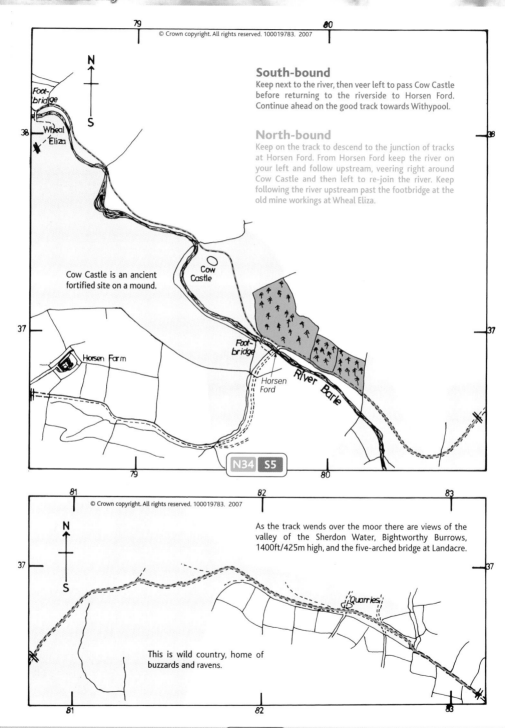

South-bound

Keep next to the river, then veer left to pass Cow Castle before returning to the riverside to Horsen Ford. Continue ahead on the good track towards Withypool.

North-bound

Keep on the track to descend to the junction of tracks at Horsen Ford. From Horsen Ford keep the river on your left and follow upstream, veering right around Cow Castle and then left to re-join the river. Keep following the river upstream past the footbridge at the old mine workings at Wheal Eliza.

Foot-bridge

Wheal Eliza

Cow Castle is an ancient fortified site on a mound.

Cow Castle

Horsen Farm

Foot-bridge

Horsen Ford

River Barle

N34 S5

As the track wends over the moor there are views of the valley of the Sherdon Water, Bightworthy Burrows, 1400ft/425m high, and the five-arched bridge at Landacre.

Quarries

This is wild country, home of buzzards and ravens.

N33 S6

See key to maps on page 7

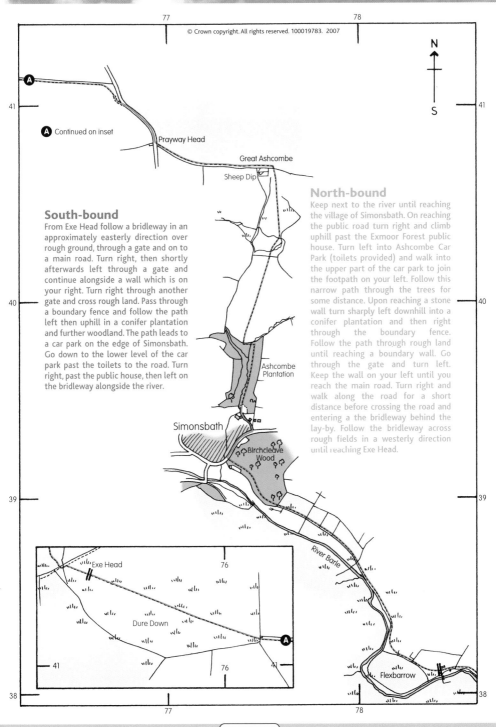

N
↑
S

A Continued on inset

Prayway Head

Great Ashcombe

Sheep Dip

South-bound

From Exe Head follow a bridleway in an approximately easterly direction over rough ground, through a gate and on to a main road. Turn right, then shortly afterwards left through a gate and continue alongside a wall which is on your right. Turn right through another gate and cross rough land. Pass through a boundary fence and follow the path left then uphill in a conifer plantation and further woodland. The path leads to a car park on the edge of Simonsbath. Go down to the lower level of the car park past the toilets to the road. Turn right, past the public house, then left on the bridleway alongside the river.

North-bound

Keep next to the river until reaching the village of Simonsbath. On reaching the public road turn right and climb uphill past the Exmoor Forest public house. Turn left into Ashcombe Car Park (toilets provided) and walk into the upper part of the car park to join the footpath on your left. Follow this narrow path through the trees for some distance. Upon reaching a stone wall turn sharply left downhill into a conifer plantation and then right through the boundary fence. Follow the path through rough land until reaching a boundary wall. Go through the gate and turn left. Keep the wall on your left until you reach the main road. Turn right and walk along the road for a short distance before crossing the road and entering a the bridleway behind the lay-by. Follow the bridleway across rough fields in a westerly direction until reaching Exe Head.

Ashcombe
Plantation

Simonsbath

Birchcleave
Wood

River Barle

Exe Head

Dure Down

Flexbarrow

Rural Buildings

The old smithy
- Ponsworthy

Granite trough and ruins
of Great Frenchbeer

Farmhouse with porch
- Dockwell

Thatched house in Drewsteignton

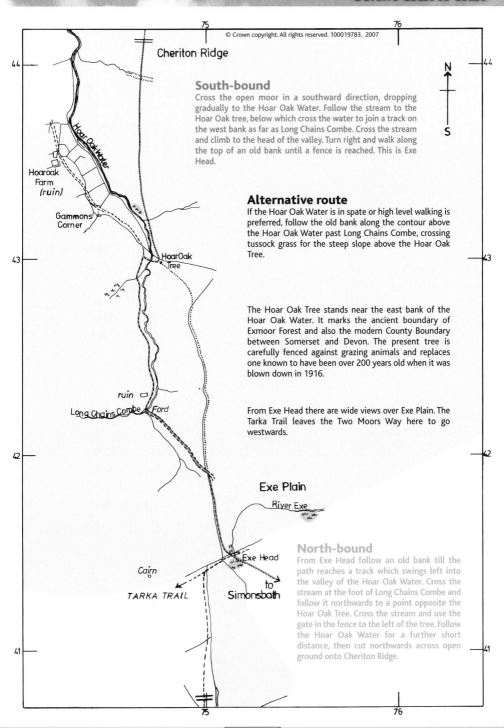

Cheriton Ridge

South-bound

Cross the open moor in a southward direction, dropping gradually to the Hoar Oak Water. Follow the stream to the Hoar Oak tree, below which cross the water to join a track on the west bank as far as Long Chains Combe. Cross the stream and climb to the head of the valley. Turn right and walk along the top of an old bank until a fence is reached. This is Exe Head.

Alternative route

If the Hoar Oak Water is in spate or high level walking is preferred, follow the old bank along the contour above the Hoar Oak Water past Long Chains Combe, crossing tussock grass for the steep slope above the Hoar Oak Tree.

The Hoar Oak Tree stands near the east bank of the Hoar Oak Water. It marks the ancient boundary of Exmoor Forest and also the modern County Boundary between Somerset and Devon. The present tree is carefully fenced against grazing animals and replaces one known to have been over 200 years old when it was blown down in 1916.

From Exe Head there are wide views over Exe Plain. The Tarka Trail leaves the Two Moors Way here to go westwards.

North-bound

From Exe Head follow an old bank till the path reaches a track which swings left into the valley of the Hoar Oak Water. Cross the stream at the foot of Long Chains Combe and follow it northwards to a point opposite the Hoar Oak Tree. Cross the stream and use the gate in the fence to the left of the tree. Follow the Hoar Oak Water for a further short distance, then cut northwards across open ground onto Cheriton Ridge.

Hoaroak Farm (ruin)

Gammons Corner

HoarOak Tree

ruin

Long Chains Combe Ford

Exe Plain

River Exe

Exe Head

Cairn

TARKA TRAIL

to Simonsbath

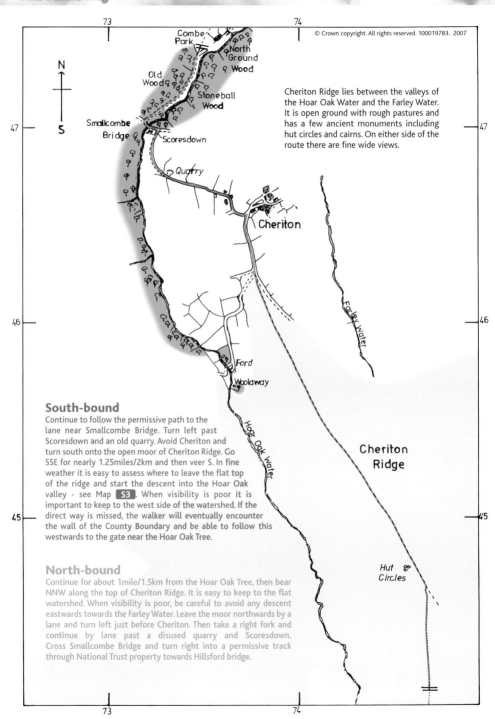

N

S

Cheriton Ridge lies between the valleys of the Hoar Oak Water and the Farley Water. It is open ground with rough pastures and has a few ancient monuments including hut circles and cairns. On either side of the route there are fine wide views.

Combe Park

North Ground Wood

Old Wood

Stoneball Wood

Smallcombe Bridge

Scoresdown

Quarry

Cheriton

Farley Water

Ford

Woolaway

Cheriton Ridge

Hoar Oak Water

Hut Circles

South-bound

Continue to follow the permissive path to the lane near Smallcombe Bridge. Turn left past Scoresdown and an old quarry. Avoid Cheriton and turn south onto the open moor of Cheriton Ridge. Go SSE for nearly 1.25miles/2km and then veer S. In fine weather it is easy to assess where to leave the flat top of the ridge and start the descent into the Hoar Oak valley - see Map **S3**. When visibility is poor it is important to keep to the west side of the watershed. If the direct way is missed, the walker will eventually encounter the wall of the County Boundary and be able to follow this westwards to the gate near the Hoar Oak Tree.

North-bound

Continue for about 1mile/1.5km from the Hoar Oak Tree, then bear NNW along the top of Cheriton Ridge. It is easy to keep to the flat watershed. When visibility is poor, be careful to avoid any descent eastwards towards the Farley Water. Leave the moor northwards by a lane and turn left just before Cheriton. Then take a right fork and continue by lane past a disused quarry and Scoresdown. Cross Smallcombe Bridge and turn right into a permissive track through National Trust property towards Hillsford bridge.

N37 S2

See key to maps on page 7

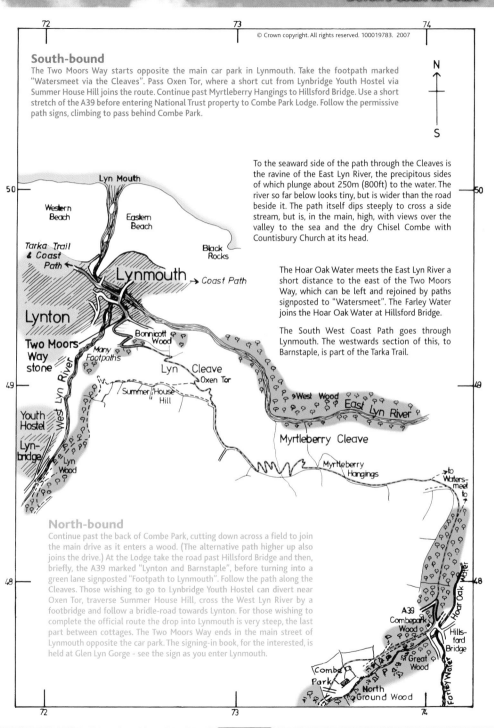

South-bound

The Two Moors Way starts opposite the main car park in Lynmouth. Take the footpath marked "Watersmeet via the Cleaves". Pass Oxen Tor, where a short cut from Lynbridge Youth Hostel via Summer House Hill joins the route. Continue past Myrtleberry Hangings to Hillsford Bridge. Use a short stretch of the A39 before entering National Trust property to Combe Park Lodge. Follow the permissive path signs, climbing to pass behind Combe Park.

To the seaward side of the path through the Cleaves is the ravine of the East Lyn River, the precipitous sides of which plunge about 250m (800ft) to the water. The river so far below looks tiny, but is wider than the road beside it. The path itself dips steeply to cross a side stream, but is, in the main, high, with views over the valley to the sea and the dry Chisel Combe with Countisbury Church at its head.

The Hoar Oak Water meets the East Lyn River a short distance to the east of the Two Moors Way, which can be left and rejoined by paths signposted to "Watersmeet". The Farley Water joins the Hoar Oak Water at Hillsford Bridge.

The South West Coast Path goes through Lynmouth. The westwards section of this, to Barnstaple, is part of the Tarka Trail.

North-bound

Continue past the back of Combe Park, cutting down across a field to join the main drive as it enters a wood. (The alternative path higher up also joins the drive.) At the Lodge take the road past Hillsford Bridge and then, briefly, the A39 marked "Lynton and Barnstaple", before turning into a green lane signposted "Footpath to Lynmouth". Follow the path along the Cleaves. Those wishing to go to Lynbridge Youth Hostel can divert near Oxen Tor, traverse Summer House Hill, cross the West Lyn River by a footbridge and follow a bridle-road towards Lynton. For those wishing to complete the official route the drop into Lynmouth is very steep, the last part between cottages. The Two Moors Way ends in the main street of Lynmouth opposite the car park. The signing-in book, for the interested, is held at Glen Lyn Gorge - see the sign as you enter Lynmouth.

Stamp of Approval

In 2006, to mark the 30th anniversary of the Two Moors Way and its extension to form the major part of Devon's Coast to Coast walk, Radio Devon (**www.bbc.co.uk/devon/local_radio**) set up a "stamp trail" covering the route. Two Radio Devon reporters, Jo Bishop and Liz Scott, walked the entire route leaving ink stamps at pubs, shops and public buildings at twelve locations along the way. Walkers can now stamp their special passport, collecting their individual stamps as they make their way along the path and if you arrive out of hours, there is an outside facility for stamps at most of the locations. By sending the completed passport to the address shown, you can then receive your special certificate. And don't forget, you don't have to walk the whole route in one chunk! You can walk sections at your leisure over a period of time.

Locations of the "stamp stations"

Wembury	Old Mill Cafe, Wembury Beach
Yealmpton	Market Street Cafe
Ivybridge	Global Travel, 19 Fore Street or Ivybridge Leisure Centre, St Leonard's Road
Holne	Holne Village Store and tearooms
Drewsteignton	Post Office Stores, The Square
Morchard Bishop	The London Inn
Witheridge	Witheridge Newsagents, 16a The Square
Knowstone	(interior) Mason's Arms (exterior) Knowstone Parish Church
West Anstey (Yeo Mill)	West Anstey Stores, Yeo Mill
Withypool	Post Office
Simonsbath	Simonsbath House Hotel
Lynmouth	Glen Lyn Gorge

Two Moors Way Association

The Two Moors Way Association supports the maintenance and promotion of the route. It holds copies of the guide book and also provides a Certificate of Achievement for all those completing the walk, price £1 including post and packing. Also available are an illustrated map (62cm x 21cm), price £2.00 and a colour badge (6cm x 8.5cm), price £1.

For any of this merchandise, a copy of the accommodation list (£2) or details of membership, contact: The Two Moors Way Association, 63 Higher Coombe Drive, Teignmouth, Devon, TQ14 9NL. Please make cheques payable to The Two Moors Way Association.

Visit the Association's website at www.twomoorsway.org.uk or email info@twomoorsway.org.uk.

You will discover more information about walking in Devon by visiting www.discoverdevon.com. By clicking the "walking" section of the website you will be able to search the walking database which details lots of ideas and information on other long-distance walks, short and circular walks, walking events, guided walks and walking holidays. The website also contains information on cycling, watersports, golf, food and drink, gardens, festivals and arts and crafts activities on offer in Devon.

Alternatively call the Discover Devon Holiday line on 0870 608 3531 (calls charged at UK national rates).

Be a Green Visitor

1. Do not disturb any livestock, keep your dog under close control and leave gates as you find them.

2. Take your litter home and recycle if possible.

3. Do not disturb wild animals, birds or flowers.

4. Whether you are walking, cycling or driving, take special care on country roads.

5. If possible, leave your car at home and take the bus. If you do bring a car, use the local car park.

6. Buy locally produced goods, including food and souvenirs. Support local shops, garages and other local services.

Devon Coast to Coast Route Overview

Coast to Coast walk route

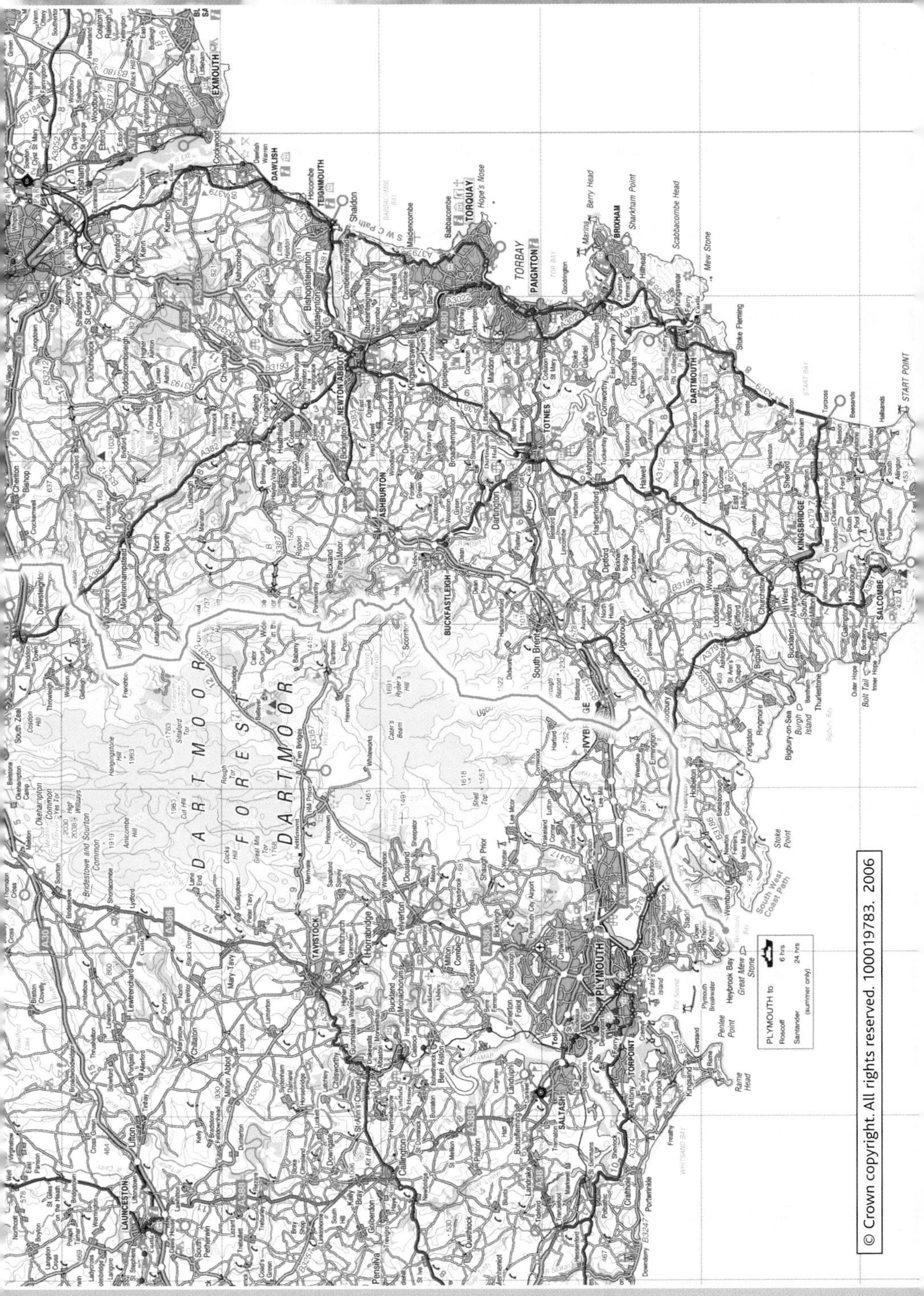
DARTMOOR
FOREST
TORBAY
EXMOUTH
DAWLISH
TEIGNMOUTH
TORQUAY
PAIGNTON
BRIXHAM
DARTMOUTH
TOTNES
NEWTON ABBOT
ASHBURTON
BUCKFASTLEIGH
KINGSBRIDGE
SALCOMBE
IVYBRIDGE
PLYMOUTH
TAVISTOCK
LAUNCESTON
SALTASH
TORPOINT
START POINT
Berry Head
Hope's Nose
Stoke Point
Rame Head
Bolt Tail
PLYMOUTH to
Roscoff 6 hrs
Santander 24 hrs
(summer only)

Fingle Bridge, Dartmoor

The Two Moors Way/Coast to Coast route is maintained and promoted by a partnership of Devon County Council, South Hams District Council and Dartmoor and Exmoor National Park Authorities. The support of Mid Devon and North Devon District Councils is also acknowledged.

The Two Moors Way has for many years received the help and support of the Two Moors Way Association. The local authorities gratefully acknowledge and value this help.